Be the Master

Fourth Edition

Don Jones

Be the Master

Fourth Edition

Don Jones

ISBN 9781670337306

Published by 25th Edition Books • 25edition.com

Also By Don Jones

The DSC Book

The PowerShell Scripting and Toolmaking Book

Become Hardcore Extreme Black Belt PowerShell Ninja Rockstar

Don Jones' PowerShell 4N00bs

Don Jones' The Cloud 4N00bs

Instructional Design for Mortals

How to Find a Wolf in Siberia

Tales of the Icelandic Troll

PowerShell by Mistake

The Culture of Learning

Be the Master

Alabaster

Let's Talk Business

Power Wave

The Never

For Jason, who made me write this.

Contents

Part V: Aspects of Mastery 101

Interlude: The Grind 135

Part VI: The Nine Rules of Life

Bonus: On Being a Better Teacher

Bonus 2: On Being a Master at Work

And, in Closing

CONTENTS

Introduction

This book started as a blog post in October 2017 on my site, DonJones.com. The post was entitled, "Become the Master, or Go Away," and it generated what was, for me, a surprising amount of attention and positive feedback. I stand by the original post to this day, but quickly realized that a more prescriptive work could also be beneficial.

First, let me explain the concept of *Master* as it exists in this book, and explain why Masters are necessary.

For thousands of years, human society has recognized that the contributions of individual human beings are important and that preserving and evolving their skills and knowledge is also important. You see signs of this recognition in our current world, such as the US patent system (as well as similar patent systems worldwide). The word *patent* is centuries old. It appeared in medieval times in phrases like *letters patent*, essentially referring to any document issued by the government that confers a right or privilege. In our modern system, a *patent* basically confers a monopoly on the manufacture and sale of a device. So why would the government offer monopolies? I mean, aren't monopolies generally to be avoided?

The answer is simple: *fear.* Fear that someone would produce an amazing invention and then *die*, leaving society unable to reproduce the invention. So a short-term monopoly was a lure for inventors to be completely candid about their invention, ensuring that society could benefit from it long into the future. You see, in order to get a patent, you have to describe exactly how it works (and you used to have to provide a working model, although not any longer). I realize that patent systems are deeply abused today, but their original intent was to protect society, not necessarily to protect the inventor.

Prior to the invention of modern patents, this same fear, this same desire to protect society, manifested itself in another way: apprenticeships. Masters in a craft—blacksmiths, for example, or carpenters—worked a lifetime to hone and perfect their trade. These craftsmen performed an invaluable service for society, which could not function without the existence of these trades. In order to preserve their livelihood, most craftsmen jealously guarded their trade secrets, their techniques, and so on. But these craftsmen were also human and subject to that ultimate human frailty— death, which resulted in the loss of that craftsman's trade secrets. And so society invented the *apprentice*. Apprentices paid a fee to join a Master's trade, and worked alongside that Master for years, learning the Master's craft and trade secrets. Eventually, an apprentice would become a *journeyman*, helping the Master increase the output of his shop, earn more business, and settle into a semi-retirement. And eventually, many journeymen would either take over the shop or leave town and set up their own shop in some other village, ultimately becoming a Master in their own right.

The important bit here is that society crafted a system that ensured the continuation and continual improvement of the trade. Yes, Masters benefitted personally from the system, just as today's patent holders do, but the *purpose* of the system was to *protect the trade*. Masters eventually ganged up to form *guilds*, which represented the interests of the trade and helped to ensure apprentices were shepherded by an accomplished Master.

So what does this mean to you?

Well, in the aforementioned blog post, I tried to make a case that we have all, at some point, been an apprentice. Most of us are at "apprentice stage" in some topic or another for most of our lives. Many of us have had the benefit of learning, at least briefly, from a "Master" in our respective trade. Too few people, however, go on to become a Master themselves. You see, the point of a Master is *not* to know it all. The point of a Master is to *teach*. To *share*. To *pass on*. When you take a class, you are paying an "apprenticeship fee" of sorts to briefly "apprentice under" a Master - the teacher of the class. But too many people let it stop there. They assume that the Master got paid, and their obligation as a student is fulfilled. But remember that the apprenticeship system, like the patent system that followed, was always meant to *protect society*. To truly be a successful apprentice, we *must* pass along what we have learned. We *must* become the Master, in at least a small way, so that we can continue sharing the information of our trades.

There's an implicit balance in this arrangement, though, that I feel needs to be made explicit: By accepting an apprentice, a Master agrees to give up some of the time normally spent in their trade. Time is money, which means the Master is agreeing to give up money—which is why, traditionally, formal apprentices paid a fee to join their Master's shop. For *you*, however, the arrangement between Master and apprentice is going to be different, and we'll come to that—because maintaining that balance between time and money is still important in our modern world.

Today, higher education—universities—have largely replaced the apprenticeship systems of old for most trades. That is a shame because a book can never capture the nuances and lore locked up in the brain of an actual practitioner. In reality, everyone who has ever been to college knows that a degree is barely the starting point; you still spend years learning your trade on the job, working alongside other journeymen and Masters. Many trades explicitly acknowledge this, requiring graduates from law school, medical school, and so on to spend time as interns—apprentices in the modern world.

Too often, we equate the term *Master* with *expert*, and we feel that, until we reach that ineffable "expert" state, we are not worthy to pass along what we know. This is bullshit. In our modern, always-connected world, *every* bit of *experience*—not knowledge, but true experience—is valuable and worthy of being passed along. Indeed, I feel we owe it to those who taught us to turn around and re-teach it, whatever "it" is, to others. As we do, we add our own experiences, our own "color," if you will. We evolve our trade, and we help ensure its survival. To not become the Master is to be a failure as an apprentice. To not become a teacher is to be selfish and to be unworthy of being taught.

There's an important point that I want to re-state: In medieval society, the position of "Master" was typically protected by a guild of some kind. You needed to *earn* your Mastery, and before you did so, you were relegated to a subservient role and not encouraged— or allowed—to pass what knowledge you *had* gained on to others. Many guilds collectively protected trade secrets, only permitting Masters to pass them on to official apprentices. In modern society, this same "privilege to teach" remains with us. University professors teach. Teachers teach. So-called "gurus" teach. Anyone not in such a privileged position simply learns. Our educational world is binary: You are either a teacher or a student. I propose that this division is ridiculous. All college professors could stand to learn a thing or two. No guru is expert in *everything*. If teaching is the act of sharing experiences, then by definition, anyone with experience can teach, and anyone who has not experienced All The Things can learn.

But again, too many of us feel that until *we* have achieved the pinnacle of "guru," we simply can't teach. Until we have become *successful*, and acknowledged by others as such, we aren't "worthy" of sharing or of teaching. I've come to find this attitude insidious and even odious. Don't get me wrong—there's a nugget of truth within it. A five-year-old child's experiences aren't necessarily fully formed enough to be considered "worth" teaching, right? But this book is for adults, and all adults, simply by virtue of having survived to be an adult, have *some* experiences worth sharing. Certainly, as you grow older and gain *more* experience and *more* context, the lessons you can teach become even more valuable. But that doesn't mean your existing experiences are *valueless*.

Here's the bar I set for myself: When I felt that I was *successful*, then I could start teaching what I'd learned. Meaning, when my aggregate experiences, knowledge, and context had grown to a sufficient degree that they had led me to a positive outcome, I was "expert enough" to share what I'd gained to that point. Now, *success*, as an old friend reminded me, is subjective, so I need to explain in more concrete terms what my "bar" was set at. For me, it meant that I and my family enjoyed comfortable shelter. We could afford to eat, and we could afford to eat out. On occasion, we could afford to eat out extravagantly. We could buy the car we wanted, and we largely wouldn't have to worry much about money unless the damn HVAC system died. I could afford to turn down jobs that didn't suit me and accept those that did. I had some say over my personal destiny. All of those are very subjective measures, ones that you can decide on for yourself. The *result* of my success has been the leisure to do some work that I *want* to do rather than only doing work that I *need* to do. Although I spend ample time with my family, and we take great vacations, my success also gives me the time to run a nonprofit that focuses on education—a personal passion. My success has, in other words, made the time for me to repay my obligation as apprentice, and to not only pass along what I've learned but help others do the same.

I realized later that I'd set the bar wrong. This wasn't actually until quite recently, when I was beginning work on the Third Edition of this book. I was working with a friend, showing him how to replace a GFCI outlet in his kitchen. Now, I'm no electrical expert, but outlets aren't terribly hard. As I pulled the old outlet out of the wall, I noticed the wires were mostly covered in paint. That's normal—when the painters come into a new house, the wires are tucked into the junction box, and the outlets themselves aren't yet installed, so the wires all get painted, too. So as I disconnected each wire, I scraped a bit of paint off so I could see the color of the insulation on the wire. My friend asked, "What're you doing?" I explained about the paint on the wires, and said it'll be easier to connect the new outlet if we could see the colors. "Oh," he said. "I didn't realize that."

That is when I realized that my bar for "Mastery" shouldn't have been some definition of my personal success, or at least not entirely. Instead, and as I'll expand on later in this book, "Mastery" came to me the moment I knew that there was some failure in my future (connecting the wires the wrong way 'round), and I almost habitually moved to mitigate that (scraping some paint off so I could see the colors). That *right there* meant I knew something useful that I could teach someone else. I might not know much else about electricity that's useful, but I know *that*, and it's worth sharing.

So sure, personal success is part of the picture, and you need to know where yours is. I realize mine isn't terribly lofty—I don't live in a mansion, I don't have a yacht, and I'm not even remotely worried about whatever the top-level tax bracket is. It's what *I* wanted, for myself and for my family. You'll need to decide what "success" looks like for you, and most importantly, you'll need to decide how to achieve it. But don't let that be your only measure. Remember, "Mastery" happens the moment you're willing to teach what you know.

This returns us to the point of balance I made earlier: Sharing what you know takes time, time that could otherwise be spent earning money or at leisure. So are you to expect to be paid for passing on your information when doing so isn't—as it is for a university professor—something you're paid for? Probably not. And in fact, if you look back at your life, many "Masters" probably helped you for free in countless ways. How did they do so? By becoming *successful* for whatever they defined as "success." Success gave them enough time to be able to spend some of it helping others, even in small ways. So *success* is part of becoming a Master, and in many ways, I feel, becoming a Master - someone who can hand down what they know—is the main reason for desiring success.

Thus, this book, or at least my hope for it. I want to share some of the attitudes and techniques that I feel have made *me* successful and taken me to a point where I personally *do* feel worthy of sharing what I've learned with others. This book describes what worked for me, in hopes that *some* small portion of it will work for *you*. My hope is to make you *feel* successful, for whatever you personally define as "success," so that you'll feel "worthy" of beginning the process of passing on what you know and have the time and space to do so. I'll try to be as prescriptive as possible so that you have some clear things to think about, or to try, as you make that journey. And I'll try to share some of what I've learned about teaching itself, in hopes that you can adapt some of it to become a superlative teacher in your own right.

I think *everyone* should become a Master in their trade, and I think everyone *can*. I think everyone, even someone with only a year or two of experience, has learned things that are worthy of sharing. I think we have a simple obligation as human beings to try and lift up those around us and those who are coming up behind us in our profession. We can all point to a guru who helped us through a difficult time or gave us insight that—even years after the fact—proved to be a turning point in our careers and lives. I think everyone should strive to do the same, to be a positive influence in our trades and in our lives. We owe it to the people who have helped *us*.

And let's be clear on something—teaching, passing on information, doesn't always feel rewarding. Ask any primary school teacher. But I don't feel that teaching *needs* to be rewarding, although for me it certainly has been on most occasions. Teaching, for *me*, is a *repayment* of something that was done for me. It's a debt that I owe, not to the person who taught me, but to the people I have yet to teach. The desire to pass on information and experience has *driven* much of my career. In technology circles, I'm a well-known instructor—teaching *is* my career in most ways. That doesn't need to be the case for everyone because in ways both large and small, we're all teachers, or can be. There's always someone with less experience and knowledge than ourselves, and it is to those people we can offer service as Master, even if only in a small way and for a brief time.

You need not agree, of course. Your definition of success may be wildly different, and the outcomes you expect from success might be entirely different. That's obviously fine—you be you. But if you've read the above and are thinking, "yeah, I kind of get that, and I want that, too," then let's get started.

The Grind

The Grind™ is a formalized version of my personal system of written exercises that I use to help keep myself on track, personally and professionally. It's how I remind myself to teach others and how I track progress toward my goals. It's a big part of this book. What I couldn't include in this book, however, was the actual write-in journal that I use as part of my own system. So I've made that available separately, in a convenient spiral-bound, large-format workbook, for those who feel it might be useful. It's available as a print-it-yourself PDF, with the option to buy a spiral-bound printed copy, for anyone who's subscribed to my mailing list at BeTheMaster.com.

Timothy the Blacksmith

This story—which is quite fictional, I assure you—encompasses every key concept in the rest of the book. This story is the book's touchstone, the place that everything ties back to. I encourage you to read it, and to be really thoughtful in that reading.

There's a story from the 1700s about a blacksmith named Timothy, from a small village not too far from Lancastershireham[^no, it's not a real place.] in some medieval European country. Timothy had joined the smithy when he was twelve and barely big enough to pick up one of the heavy hammers his Master (who is not named in the story) beat metal with. His first tasks were largely custodial—sweeping out the shop, keeping the forge hot, and so on. Eventually, he was given small errands to run around the village, such as delivering finished goods to customers. By age seventeen, he'd grown enough to swing the hammers himself, and he helped his Master with basic pieces. By twenty, he was working on his own for many basic projects—horseshoes were in particular demand, and this smithy was known for the unique, hoof-saving designs that Timothy's Master had taught him.

By twenty-five, he and his Master were working side by side. Together, they'd been able to take on larger and more complex projects than the Master could have handled alone, and the smithy prospered. Timothy had begun to fiddle around with some designs of his own, including complex iron padlocks, which were relatively new for their village.

One day, Timothy's Master was watching him pour a small ladle of molten metal into a mold. Timothy was moving incredibly slowly, and his Master could see the metal already starting to cool before it was in the mold. "You're moving too slowly," he noted. "I'm trying not to drop it!" Timothy replied. His Master picked up an iron poker that had been leaning against the side of the forge, walked over to Timothy, and knocked the ladle out of his hands. Molten metal spilled onto the dirt floor of the smithy. "Hey!" Timothy cried. "Now that that's over," his Master said, replacing the poker, "can we get on with it?"

When Timothy was twenty-eight (and married, with two lovely, small children and a small house of his own), a few years after his Master had officially declared him a journeyman, his Master took on a new apprentice. At first, Timothy was relieved because he'd still been stuck doing all the manual chores that his Master didn't want to do, and a decade-plus of sweeping was starting to wear thin. The new apprentice was named Edmund, and he quickly started to take on the lowest of Timothy's tasks.

As Edmund grew, their Master had him work closely with Timothy to learn the craft. The Master still took on most of Edmund's education, but Timothy discovered that Edmund loved to cast small parts, and the two of them began to work together on ever-more-complex padlocks, in addition to the smithy's continuing large output of horseshoes. In fact, Edmund through sheer accident discovered a technique for casting smaller parts with more precision, a technique he shared, with all the excitement of his youth, with Timothy. The two of them immediately devised a new lock design that took advantage of the new casting technique.

By the time Edmund was sixteen, Timothy was thirty-two and their Master was pushing fifty. The Master had, in the past couple of years, gotten a bit frail. Some days, he wouldn't come into the smithy at all, letting Timothy deal with customers, orders, and with Edmund. After a couple of years of essentially running the smithy himself on top of educating Edmund, Timothy was thinking about moving to a village that didn't have a blacksmith and setting up his own smithy. After all, if he was going to do all of the work, why not keep all of the income? But he'd grown to love his Master, and his family was thriving in the village, so leaving was difficult. Timothy decided to confront his Master about it.

"Master," he said, "I feel as if you're taking advantage of me. I run the smithy, I negotiate with our customers, I produce the majority of the work, and we rarely collaborate any more. Edmund helps on the larger pieces now."

His Master nodded. "That is as it should be. I built this business myself when I was young, and much of our trade comes from the reputation I began. You are a journeyman, and your share of the smithy's profits are appropriate to your station."

Timothy took a moment to calm himself. "I know, Master, and I do not disagree. But *you* are the Master, here, not I. So why am I also tasked with teaching our trade to Edmund, if I am only a journeyman?"

The Master paused for a moment. "I understand. Before I answer you, though, I have a question: Do you feel you're doing a good job educating Edmund?"

Timothy thought about it. "I do. He's really coming along, and he's making a number of smaller pieces on his own. And I do enjoy working with him and teaching him."

His Master smiled. "A journeyman must do two things. The first is to obey his Master, which you have done, though I have asked much of you. The second is to learn when he is the Master." His Master handed Timothy his keys to the smithy. "It took you a couple of years longer than I thought, Master Blacksmith, but now I can retire."

Timothy objected. "Master," he said, "I'm honored that you think I'm ready, but there's still so much I don't know. I'm not ready to be Master, yet."

His Master snorted. "I never could make a proper shield," he said, and walked out.

Part I: What We Get Wrong

Most cultures nowadays don't set us up to succeed—for any definition of success. We've got some broken attitudes, and things we just plain get wrong. It's time to face up to them, set them aside, and move on.

Education

Most people I've met have a fairly toxic relationship with *education*. Now, I'll mention that to people I meet sometimes, and they'll often say something like, "no, I enjoyed school, it was fine," which actually illustrates the problem: we think of *education* as being exclusively *school*.

I get why: for most of us, school is one of the first experiences we remember outside the home. When you're in kindergarten or first grade, your teacher certainly isn't interested in things like your opinion on a subject. Sure, teachers may encourage *discussion*, but throughout our primary education experience, teachers are authority figures, and students are by and large expected to do what the teachers tell them.

For those who move into university settings, the situation doesn't change much. Professors make it clear who's in charge, and who's smarter than who. Students are there to learn, and perhaps to *participate*, but the students aren't there to teach.

Many of us move on to careers where continuing education plays at least a small role. We're sent to class for a week to learn a new skill, a new process, a new technology, or whatever. Again, students are encouraged to *participate* in the class, but they're not expected to *contribute* to other students' learning. Indeed, the standard "script" for someone teaching adults is to introduce themselves, and then go over their qualifications to establish themselves as an authority. I was literally taught to do that when I received my first technology "Train the Trainer" certification.

All of this creates an enormous toxicity around the concept of education. We're taught that you are either a teacher or a student; the idea of being both at the same time is never brought to our attention. We're taught that being a teacher confers authority, and that only people with "good enough" credentials can hold that authority. Most importantly, most of us as adult human beings never have a moment where someone says, "okay, you're good enough now." Teaching is held to be the domain of people who basically do it for a living; anyone else can't be a teacher. Teaching is something that happens in set-aside environments and times: in classrooms, during classes.

It's all a lie.

Classic apprenticeships often include classroom time, of course, but they *mostly* consists of time spent on the job, where apprentices work directly with the Masters who are teaching them. Learning isn't something that happens only in a specific time or place; it can happen *always*. Making a mistake on the job is a form of learning, provided you can learn from the mistake.

All of us have something that we're "worthy" to teach. Ever taught your kid to make scrambled eggs, or to ride a bike? You were Master to their apprentice. Every walk through a process of some kind with someone new at work? Master to apprentice. Teaching, and learning, happens around us all the time. And once you set aside your toxic assumptions about education, you realize that Masters can easily learn something from their apprentices, even while teaching them:

As Edmund grew, their Master had him work closely with Timothy to learn the craft. The Master still took on most of Edmund's education, but Timothy discovered that Edmund loved to cast small parts, and the two of them began to work together on ever-more-complex padlocks, in addition to the smithy's continuing large output of horseshoes. In fact, Edmund through sheer accident discovered a technique for casting smaller parts with more precision, a technique he shared, with all the excitement of his youth, with Timothy. The two of them immediately devised a new lock design that took advantage of the new casting technique.

In medieval times, we relied upon the Master-apprentice system for most of the world's practical education. Sure, the rich kids may have gone off to a nascent Oxford to learn philosophy and such, but they were *mainly* going meet the other rich kids and develop their social network. The real work in the world was being done by craftsmen, and the real education in the world has happening between them and their apprentices.

It was relatively recently that we turned education entirely over to academia. Compulsory formal education didn't start in the United States until the mid-1600s; the expectation in the United States that every kid would attend college didn't become a thing until the late 1960s. Today, a four-year degree is considered table stakes by many people, and it's hard to find many professional-level jobs that don't mandate a "four-year degree or equivalent experience." We've put an enormous amount of faith and value into formal education, and whether that's right or wrong, it means we've stopped thinking of any other type of education as valuable.

It also means that we tend to think of learning and teaching only applying to the things we've been formally educated on. I have people tell me all the time, "well, it's not like teaching your kid to ride a bike is *teaching*." Well, it *is*—you even said the word "teaching!" People don't regard that as teaching because it didn't happen in the context of a formal education environment.

In the business world, we often try to disguise non-formal teaching as something else. The word *mentor* gets used a lot in the United States. Mentor is actually the name of a character in the Odyssey; he *taught* Telemachus, the son of Odysseus. So saying you're "mentoring someone" is a lot like saying you're "rogering someone," in that you've turned a person's name into a verb. My British friends find that comparison very amusing, by the way. No, you're not "mentoring;" you're *teaching*. Maybe for whatever reason isn't uncomfortable to use words like "Master" and "apprentice," or you live someplace where the title "teacher" is controlled by law, but just internally acknowledge that's what it is.

Even when I talk to people who set aside all the biases about education that they've been handed, they'll say things like, "I *do* want to teach people, but what can I teach them? Everyone else at work already knows everything we need to know." Again, that's leaning heavily on some bad ideas about education. *Everything you know* is worth teaching, whether it is a "big topic" like you might need to know at work, or a "little topic" that "merely" helps someone get through life.

I have a 40-year old friend who literally did not know what a credit rating was, or how it affected their life, or how they could monitor and control it. They were aware of the *existence* of them, but largely unaware, for example, that having twenty open credit cards could negatively impact that rating. They had no concept of the idea of "credit" as a thing you had a limited amount of, and could run out of. That friend decided to apply for a mortgage, and we had to have some fairly long conversations about how credit works. I wasn't a "teacher" in the formal sense, and we certainly didn't go to a classroom. In a small sense, I was acting as Master to their apprentice in a small, constrained topical area. Knowledge was shared in a practical, casual manner. Learning occurred.

The point here is to not underestimate your value as a teacher, and to not underestimate the value of *everything* you know or have learned over the years. Honestly, if we all spent more time being mini-Masters to a variety of mini-apprentices all around us, *everyone* would likely be better off.

We inherit a lot of bad ideas about education from the way our culture has evolved around it:

- You're not "good enough" to teach unless you've been conferred with a special title or position that delivers knowledge.
- Learning happens in set-aside times, in special set-aside environments like classrooms.
- Only things taught in a formal setting, like a college, are subjects worthy of being taught.

Success

Success, for me, is an even stranger and less-healthy concept than education. With education, I feel our culture has handed us a pretty concrete definition of what that culture thinks education is. Mind you, I think it's a terrible definition, but it's at least a concrete thing you can stand up, look at, throw rocks at, and break down.

Success is stranger in that we're all told it's a good thing, we all want it somehow, but nobody knows what it is. Some people get so sick of it that they'll say things like, "oh, I don't even worry about success," which is sad to me. I've come to view success as the means by which I'll live my life; to not worry about success is to not worry about my life, which would be a horrible situation.

Ask most people on the street what "success" is, and they'll usually have an answer that connects to money and/or job title. Ask them to really pin it down, and most people might offer a salary number, or describe the type of house you could afford, or point to a luxury car passing on the street. They're not entirely *wrong*, but they're missing the point.

The first thing to recognize is that "success," as a standalone concept, *means nothing*. It literally has no definition. I went to Dictionary.com, and the definition reads:

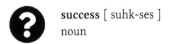 **success** [suhk-ses]
noun

1. the favorable or prosperous termination of attempts or endeavors; the accomplishment of one's goals.
2. the attainment of wealth, position, honors, or the like.
3. a performance or achievement that is marked by success, as by the attainment of honors:
4. a person or thing that has had success, as measured by attainment of goals, wealth, etc.:

Two of those definitions *use the word success in the defintion.* "Success is a performance that is marked by success." How exactly am I supposed to evaluate that? "Success is the attainment of wealth, position, honors, and such." Okay... how much? How much wealth is "success?" What is "wealth?"

You see the problem. We're all more or less coached to believe success is desirable—and it is!—but we're not actually told what it is. And this is where the "rat race" comes from. We just start chasing "more" and "better." More salary. Better title. More whatever. Better whatever. We keep striving for success, but we have no way of knowing when we've made it.

I did a survey for this edition of the book. 723 people responded to two simple questions:

- Are you at a comfortable place in life?
- Are you successful?

91% responded "yes" to the first question. 12% responded "yes" to the second.

If you are comfortable in your life, how is that not successful?

In prior editions of this book, I advised readers to stat by defining what success means to them, and you're going to go through that exercise in this edition as well. But my view of success, and what it actually is for, has evolved a bit. In this edition, you're going to define what success means *as your third step.* Because I've realized what the actual definition of success is. Perhaps I'll submit this to Dictionary.com:

success [suhk-ses]
noun
5. the state of a career that is able to provide you with the life that you desire.

Once your career is supporting the life you want, *you are successful.* You may exit the rat race, with everyone's blessing. You may, at that point, fall back to making sure your career is *sustainable,* but you no longer need to make it *better* or *more* somehow. You made it.

If the point of being alive, for you, is to live the life that you want with the family and friends that you desire, then the point of your career is to make that possible. Once it has, you're successful. This is going to be a big point of this book, because realizing that success *can* be defined, that *you* get to define it, and that success has a firm and actual *purpose* in life, is how you set yourself free. It's how you give yourself more time. And it's how you can start making the time and space to help other people.

Heroes and Role Models

Another relationship that I think we need to re-think—in addition to success and education—is the relationship we have with our heroes and role models.

The problem with people we admire, especially the ones we admire from afar, is that we never see the full package. At best, we see a limited, public-facing subset of who that person is; at worst, we see a carefully packaged facade designed to hide the real person. Take Hollywood actors, rock stars, or any other famous person: you can love 'em and appreciate 'em, but your'e going to be shocked when they turn out to be a thief, sexual assailant, or political ideologue.

Heroes and role models, for those who admire them, aren't people, they're archetypes. They're a thing we might aspire to be, but again: the problem is that we're only aspiring to be the bits we *see*. People are a package deal, though, and you can't only be the good-looking bits.

Here's why I think this is important: it's easy for a lot of us to get stuck in the rut of, "I can't really offer anything valuable to anyone else. I mean, look at (insert name of role model)! I learned from them, and I'm nowhere near as good as they are!" That attitude is a toxic dead-end. What you should say, when you think something like that is, "...I learned from them, and I don't perceive myself to be as good as I perceive them to be, but honestly I don't know them all that well and I could in fact be smarter than them in a hundred ways."

I'll offer a personal anecdote.

I'm well-known in the world of Windows PowerShell, a technology made by Microsoft to help automate the administration and operations of computer servers. PowerShell is sort of a programming language with a very specific purpose, and it's not the easiest thing in the world to learn. I got to be well-known because I wrote two of the first books about it, spoke at conferences about it for over a decade, wrote what may be the best-selling entry-level book on the topic, and received ten awards from Microsoft recognizing my contributions to the community. People *do* look at me and think, "well, I learned PowerShell from Don, and I'm nowhere near as smart as he is with it, so how could I possibly help someone else?"

Here's what you don't know about me: *I'm not an expert in PowerShell.* If PowerShell expertise could be expressed on a scale of 1 to 100, I'd be maybe a 40. People *perceive* me as an expert because I was probably one of the people they learned from when they were just getting started. What they don't realize is that I know *nothing* to *very little* about the more complex bits of PowerShell. I'm simply *really* good at explaining the basics. My book didn't sell well because it made you an expert; it sold well because it did a good job of teaching you the basics. There are tons of people who've gone way past the basics, yet *still* feel they're not "worthy" of teaching the basics.

Don't try to impress your heroes. Don't try to become a person your role models would admire. Thank them for whatever they've done for you or inspired you to do, and then *go impress someone else.* Someone who actually needs you. Forget your role models, and go *be a role model* instead.

A lot of people do the same thing at the gym. They make that New Year's resolution, buy a membership, and hit the gym hard in January. But the whole time they're there, they're eyeing that buff guy on the squat rack, or that slim lady on the spin bike. *I can't be like that,* they'll think to themselves, and then they gradually come to see the gym as pointless and stop going. I'm not saying that's the only challenge with gyms, or that everyone takes that attitude, but for people who *do,* you kind of have to point out *all the other people in the gym.* My gym has some incredibly fit, and attractive people, and I started in the same place of, "I can't be that." But my trainer grabbed me and turned me around, and pointed at the *other* people in the room. The people who were older than me, struggling with more weight than I was, dealing with physical injuries I didn't have. He pointed to them and said, "why don't you get yourself to a point where you could just help one of them, and forget the people who might not need your help?" It was a very mind-opening moment.

Don't measure yourself against someone you consider to be the best in the room; measure yourself in the lives you've helped.

Part II: Realize Your Worth

We've all had that feeling of, "I'm not worthy," especially when it comes to the topic of helping other people. But I'm going to prove to you that you're wrong—you've been worthy all along.

What is "Worth?"

The first big lesson in this book is "You are Worthy," which means we need to take a hard look at what "worth" is. Unfortunately, it's a little like success: worth is subjective, and there's no concrete definition for it that you can measure yourself again.

From Dictionary.com:

worth [wurth]
preposition

1. good or important enough to justify (what is specified)
2. having a value of, or equal in value to, as in money

noun

3. excellence of character or quality as commanding esteem
4. usefulness or importance, as to the world, to a person, or for a purpose
5. value, as in money.
6. a quantity of something of a specified value

Not a lot of help, there. "Good or important enough..." For what? "Usefulness or importance, as to the world, to a person." Well, maybe we have something there.

Are you "useful or important to a person?" Not the person you admire most, but to *anyone*.

I want to revisit the story from the previous chapter, about my personal trainer back in the day. In a way, that personal trainer was a role model for me for a time. He was fit, good-looking, and friendly. He was comfortable in the gym, a place I was deeply terrified of. He could pick up *very* heavy things, put them back down, and not crack in half. But he was not *globally better than me.* I knew how to run a business. I knew how to operate a computer like nobody's business. I was an accomplished, published author. I ran my own business and made decent money at it. He couldn't do any of those things.

That didn't mean either of us was "worth" more than the other. To his clients, he was worth more than me. To *my* clients, I was worth more than him. Worth is subjective and contextual; your worth depends on who you're talking to, and what you're talking to them about. If you need to learn the basics of a technology called Windows PowerShell, Don Jones might be worth a lot to you. If you need to do the engineering on an architectural blueprint before building a house, Don Jones is worth little more than being able to get you a beer while the engineer does the math.

Our concept of "worth" tends to be very connected to our heroes and role models: we want to be like them, and so we weigh our worth against *how we value them.* It's like we want to have the same level of worth that they do, to the same people they do. But that's logically impossible. I can never have a worth that is equal, *to me,* as the worth of my trainer is *to me.* In other words, I will never be as good a trainer to me as my trainer was to me. But that doesn't mean I can't be of some worth to someone else.

Another, more heavy-handed way to think about your worth is to compare it to money. Money is only valuable when (a) someone has it, and (b) someone else wants it. If I want a gallon of milk and you have a gallon of milk, and if I have $4.00 and you want $4.00, and if you're willing to exchange your milk for my money, then we've agreed on the *worth* of both the money and the milk.

So if you *have something* that someone else wants, then *you are worthy to them.* If they have something you want, then *they are worthy to you.* And if the two of you agree that the value of those things is equal, then you can exchange them. For them, they might want your knowledge. For you, you might simply enjoy sharing it, meaning the "thing of worth" that they have to offer is their *attention.* You exchange those two, and you've struck a bargain.

Worth is defined *by the recipient.* So don't ever tell yourself that "you're not worthy." You are; perhaps you simply haven't found the right recipient of your worth. You're ready to be a Master, but you've simply not found your apprentice.

A Diversity of Perspective

We hear a lot today about *diversity*. Companies get lambasted for not being diverse enough, and entire industries make pledges to become more diverse.

I often talk to people who're looking for ways to "give back" to whatever communities they're a part of, and the single most common objection–and we're talking, like, 90% of people saying this–is that "everything's already been done." Meaning, "I want to share with people, but everything I feel I can share has already been shared by the person *I* learned it from, so why bother repeating it?"

Because of *diversity*.

When I talk about computer stuff, I tend to create analogies that have to do with automobiles. There's very little in the world of computers I can't explain by using a car analogy. Cars are reasonably universal, and most people understand enough about them for the analogies to work.

But what about the people who don't?

I also use a lot of house-construction analogies. I've been involved in that activity enough that I understand it, and it offers simple parallels that help explain complex concepts.

But what about the people who've never seen a house being built?

The point is that I teach *from my perspective*. I have to, because it's really the only one I've got. But it's not helpful when my perspective, and that of a learner, doesn't overlap in any way.

Learning, from the perspective of cognitive science, is where your brain ingests knowledge along with sensory input like sounds and smells. It creates a network of neurons that all fire together. Memories and situations play into those networks, as well, so that when a given situation happens to you again, that network lights up and solutions and advice and other information are all instantly available. The process of connecting all that stuff together is called *synthesis*, and everyone's brain does it in a slightly different way. That difference–that *diversity*–makes everyone's "take" on a subject uniquely valuable. Someone who's led a life similar to yours, and who has experienced situations similar to yours, will learn more readily from *your* teaching than from mine. The language you use, the analogies you create, even the way you sequence the material, will make a great deal of difference to different people.

"Edmund," Timothy asked, "what's the matter?" Edmund had been struggling with horseshoes all morning, and almost all of his had turned out too brittle to actually use.

"I keep trying," the boy complained, "and I keep doing it the way Master showed me, but they keep coming out this way."

Timothy nodded. "Yeah, I had that problem too. You know that bit he does where he kind of twirls the ladle as he's pulling the molten metal out of the crucible?" Edmund nodded. "I think he's a bit rheumy in that shoulder, honestly," Timothy continued. "And that twist makes it easier for him. I could never get it, though. I just kind of dip it in," and he demonstrated his technique to Edmund, "and back out again all in one go. You end up with enough hot material at the top to hold until you get it to the mold."

Edmund's eyes lit up. "So it's just about keeping the freshest stuff at the top?"

Timothy nodded again. "Yeah, basically. And then just swing it right to the mold and dump it in. Works for me almost every time."

"Thank you!"

So it *is* worth "re-teaching" the same thing over and over, provided different people are doing it from their different perspectives. Teaching is little more than taking something *that a bunch of people already know*, and then re-packaging it for a different audience. *Your* audience. Sure, that means we'll have eleventeen different versions of something out there, but that's *ideal.* Each version is like its own little genome, and the ones that provide value to the world will thrive. They'll teach and inspire new people, who'll turn around and make their own version.

Your *worth* as a Master does not lie in your ability to teach exactly like others have. Your worth comes from your apprentices; if you can explain something to someone, then to them, you're worthy.

So just because you learned something doesn't mean it's not worth re-teaching, in your own voice, in your own way, using your own process. Every Master is different, and that difference itself is where the value lies.

Knowing it All

There's a perception that you're not "good enough" to teach until you know everything. Indeed, as I'll point out later, adult education often starts with the premise that instructors must establish their superior knowledge in order to maintain authority over the class. As in Timothy's story, however, a moment's thought will show this theory to be false. Nobody knows everything, ergo, you know *something* that someone else doesn't. It's just a matter of finding them, and teaching them; you don't need to be an "expert" in order to share knowledge.

This brings up another point of imposter syndrome that I'd like to dig into because it's something that really held *me* back for years. My problem had to do with what I call *observational bias*.

Hop onto your favorite news website and tell me—based entirely on the data you see there—how you think your town, your region, your country, or the entire world is doing. "Not so well," is a likely answer, because news media rarely publishes stories with headlines like, "Nothing Bad Happened Today." Apart from one instance on April 18, 1930, when the BBC announced that it had, in fact, "no news," I'm not sure it's *ever* happened. This is observational bias: you observe only a limited set of available data, and you draw erroneous conclusions from it.

Imposter syndrome comes from the same place. We tend to look at our "gurus," our *exemplars*, the people *we* learn from, and gauge ourselves against them. If we're not as smart as we perceive *them* to be, then we're not ready to teach. And many of us work in environments full of intelligent, capable people—and again, we compare ourselves to *them*. Surely if we're not at least *that* good, then we've no business teaching someone else anything, right? But that's observational bias. Look *further*. Look outside your usual environment. Look at those other than your "gurus." Due to a biological phenomenon called the "birth rate," there are *always* people with less knowledge and experience than you. Seek them out, and teach *them*. As adults in the modern world, our apprentices aren't going to approach us and pay a fee for lifelong career training; we need to find our own audience, and help them as much as we can.

Remember, to be a Master is *not* to know it all—even if you can't forge a proper shield, you probably have plenty to teach and share.

Incidentally, be prepared for the fact that stuff you personally find interesting and fun and leading-edge might *not* be the best way to help others. Take my career: I'm known, in my industry, for teaching what amounts to a programming language. Like many things technological, it includes a spectrum of things, some more entry-level and others much more advanced. The advanced stuff, to me, is cool. It's hard, like a puzzle, and I enjoy playing with it. But that's not what I teach. I teach entry-level stuff, because the entry-level people are the ones who need the most help. Folks interested in the super-hard stuff have already made it far enough that they can figure it out on their own—they don't *need* me. So what I teach isn't necessarily the same as what personally fascinates me. I'm not known as a "hardcore" technical guy in my field—I'm known as a decent teacher. I mean, it'd be lovely to have a reputation of knowing everything about the technology I love—but it's even more lovely to know I've helped bring so many people into it to begin with.

Confidence vs. Arrogance

Most people I've met (certainly not all, but most) are pretty down-to-earth, humble people. I don't know a lot of people who'd stand on a street corner and criticize the clothing of passersby, however fun that might be to watch. Certainly, we see a lot of that on television, but in real life it's relatively rare.

Humble people are, by definition, pretty careful not to be arrogant. Arrogance is not the way to win friends and influence enemies; it's a way to annoy people and isolate yourself. But humility can go too far.

To keep things simple and easy to talk about, I like to say that *confidence* is knowing what you know and not being ashamed of it. If you can fix a car, it's okay to just say so. *Arrogance* is knowing less than you present yourself as knowing; it's saying you can fix any car in ten minutes when that isn't at all the truth. There is obviously a hair-thin line between arrogance and confidence, and so most of us will err on the side of caution and understate ourselves. Rather than saying, "Yeah, I can absolutely fix that jammed garbage disposal," many of us will temporize with, "Well, I mean, I can take a look—that happened to me once and it might be the same thing." There's nothing at all wrong with that, by the way, and I don't want to give you the impression that I disapprove. But recognizing that most of us are uncomfortable getting too close to that line between *arrogance* and *confidence* is important.

It's difficult to teach when you're not confident of what you're teaching, especially among adults. You worry that you'll say something and get called on it. "Hey, stove tops designed for natural gas can absolutely be converted to run on propane, and it's a dead-easy change," you might say—and then nervously eye the other cooking appliance professionals in the room to make sure nobody disagrees. Or, if you're just an iota less confident, you simply say nothing. After all, you don't want to seem arrogant.

Worse is the *completeness* that we demand of our confidence. I wouldn't *dream* of teaching a class on advanced computer programming. Don't get me wrong—I can write computer code. I can do it in six or seven different languages. I'd just be terrified that someone in my class would ask me something *I didn't know* and make me look like an idiot, right when I'm trying to win the confidence of my students. In other words, unless we feel we know *everything* about our topic, we won't teach *anything* about it, just in case someone finds a gap in our knowledge and we look stupid. *I don't know everything about computer programming, so it'd be arrogant to teach a class on it.*

Fun fact worth repeating: Nobody knows everything about anything. I work in the technology industry, and since 2006 have worked with a Microsoft product called PowerShell (that's the programming language I mentioned earlier). I've become good friends with the guy who invented the technology, and with several of the people who initially created it. I absolutely know things about the technology *that they do not,* and they've said so. Obviously, they know tons about it that I don't. And *that's fine.*

I trace this confidence problem right back to formal learning, again, where we establish some kind of wolf pack-style hierarchy of dominance with the instructor as top dog. "As the instructor, I must establish and maintain my authority to teach this class or you might not want to learn from me; if you discover a gap in my knowledge, then I fall from my mountain and the entire world falls apart. Ergo, I will not teach unless I know everything." This is, and pardon my intensity here, bullshit. If we instead approach learning as a *collaboration*—hey, I don't know it all, but I've got some stuff that you might want to know—then we immediately leave room for our own failings to coexist peacefully with our strengths.

Timothy's Master made *horseshoes.* Even in the 1700s, this was not a complex technology. Nobody ever said he knew how to craft *all things* using a forge. Nothing in the story, for example, said a word about making spears, swords, and armor, which is what we typically envision a blacksmith making, and he admitted his lack of skill in making something as seemingly simple as a shield. He was a Master of his trade, not the omniscient God of it. He had plenty to teach Timothy and Edmund, but that didn't mean he didn't have plenty that he could learn from others. Young Edmund discovered a new casting technique that he shared with Timothy—and it didn't get Timothy demoted back to apprentice for not knowing *everything* there was to know; they simply used the new information and moved on.

You do not need to be an *expert* to be a Master. A Master is someone who shares information with those who need it; that does not imply Total World Dominance of the topic. Don't fear not knowing, and don't set up relationships that rely on some unattainable absolute supremacy of knowledge. Don't let all your formal learning experiences shape how you share information with others. Becoming the Master doesn't mean placing yourself *above* anyone. You can be the Master to an apprentice today, and that same apprentice can be Master tomorrow. It's about *sharing your craft,* whether in small, personal bites or in large groups.

Remember:

Timothy objected. "Master," he said, "I'm honored that you think I'm ready, but there's still so much I don't know. I'm not ready to be Master, yet."

His Master snorted. "I never could make a proper shield," he said, and walked out.

Failure and Fear

Fear is a powerful motivator, and an equally powerful de-motivator. And because our monkey brains still lurk underneath our modern facade, we know that *failure* often means *death*. That makes a fear of failure pretty strong.

Sometimes, you have to recognize that your biology works against you. Your brain, for example, is hardwired in such a way that *the fear of losing something* is about three times more emotionally powerful than the reward feeling you get by gaining something or succeeding. "A bird in hand is worth two in the bush" is literally coded into your DNA.

People will use this against you, and you can use it against yourself.

Fear of moving to a different city. Fear of a foreigner taking a job. Fear of missing out on something. *Fear* is one of the strongest human motivators. You could definitely prove to someone that— to take an extreme example—more foreigners open businesses and hire people than foreigners take jobs from natives, and most people would not be able to accept the fact. Their *belief*—their *fear*—would override the fact and override the idea that having a foreigner around might create more job opportunities.

You have to recognize the ways in which fear is used to influence your life and the degree to which this fear is hardcoded into your brain. You will make instinctive, gut-level decisions before your conscious mind even realizes something is happening, and those decisions are *really hard* to get out of your mind once they're made.

This fear of loss keeps people in jobs they hate. It keeps people in relationships that are toxic. It makes them vote for terrible politicians. *Most* bad human decisions, in my experience, boil down to fear. If you're going to succeed, if you're going to rise above, if you're going to *conquer* your life and truly become a driver rather than a passenger, you have to work past this fear. You have to acknowledge that you can't just "let it go" because it's baked into who you are. You can't ignore it because it will influence your mind whether you pay attention or not. You have to *face* that fear, analyze it, confront it, and set it aside.

You cannot *not* be afraid. You have to *be afraid* and move on anyway. This is hard. This is worth it. Much of my success has come from doing things that worked out but were terrifying at the time. Conversely, many of the biggest opportunities I missed out on were due entirely to my fear of trying.

There's a funny and uncomfortable truth about human beings that is in direct contradiction to how we'd normally prefer to live.

On the one hand, none of us likes to look stupid. "Not looking stupid" usually entails "not screwing up," which if we can just trim that down to a concise two-word statement, means "don't fail."

On the other hand, failure is really the only way we learn. Our entire system of science is based on stating a hypothesis and then experimenting to see if we can prove it, except that we more often end up disproving bits of it. Failure is how we create new knowledge. You've seen this with kids: Tell a kid not to touch the hot pot on the stove, and the kid is all but *guaranteed* to do exactly that. Once, usually, because ouch. But then they learn—and they don't make that mistake again, right? Well, I mean the smart ones.

Anyway, it's sometimes amazing to watch how deeply our fear of failure embeds itself in our brains. For example, when I'm teaching a technology class, we have a room with maybe a dozen people, each with their own computer. These computers are running special software that literally is designed to let you experiment, break things, and then almost instantly "reset" the computer to its original condition. No muss, no fuss. But I'll *always* have students asking, "Well, what happens if I do XXX?" WHY ARE YOU NOT JUST TRYING IT? I mean, you're literally *in a lab environment* with zero possible negative consequences! But that fear of failure is *really deep.*

I also write course books that are used in these technical classes, which are taught by other people. A hallmark of most technology courses is the Lab Guide, which tells students what to do when the lecture ends and it's time to try out some of what they've just learned. *My* Lab Guides provide a clear set of goals along with a refresh of what the student has done previously to help them maintain context. I'll often provide a kind of "starting point" for students who perhaps didn't have time to complete an earlier lab. The main complaint I get is that the Lab Guide doesn't include detailed, numbered, step-by-step instructions for completing the lab. That's because some students are *so afraid of failure* that they won't even take a stab at completing a lab that requires independent thought. Basically, "let's just forget that this is a class and pretend I'm a lightly trained monkey—what do you want me to do?" Like, am I also supposed to go home with you, and provide detailed steps for whatever it is you do *for a living?* When this fear of failure sabotages *your own ability to learn,* then ... I mean ... what good are you?

"Just be careful," Timothy's Master warned, "not to drip any water into the mold after it's gotten hot. Sometimes the metal will look cool, but always test it with just a small drop before you pour the whole cup."

"What will happen?" young Timothy asked.

His Master shrugged. "I don't know," he said. "Maybe it's just something I was told by my Master. Why don't you give it a try?"

Timothy, suspecting a trick, just stared back, but the Master gestured toward the mold, just filled with molten metal and only beginning to cool. Timothy picked up a small bucket of water and poured it over the hot mold. Water flashed into steam, stinging his hands. A sharp *crack* resounded through the smithy, and Timothy looked down to see the mold split in three, still-warm metal sluggishly pooling out onto the workbench.

"I guess that's what happens," his Master said. "At least now we know."

The whole Facebook motto of "Move fast and break things" is an explicit corporate acknowledgement that *we're not going to get it right every time*. Instead, these newer Internet companies aim to make their mistakes quickly, recover from them just as quickly, and move on. Get the learning out of the way, *learn* the lesson, *apply* the lesson, and on to the next thing. They've tried to reduce or eliminate the fear of failure, knowing that failure is the thing that actually moves you forward. *Not* failing is the same as standing still.

Think about that. What have you *not* done because you were afraid you'd fail? As I write this, I'm about to make a pretty significant real estate investment so that I can own rental property. I have been a landlord exactly zero times. I know very little about it, apart from the great stuff I've read on the Internet, all of which is true. This is a *real* amount of money I stand to lose. Sure, I could just dump that money into a savings account and rake in the massive .01% interest or whatever, but I'm trying to "do the right thing" and diversify where my money is working for me. Owning real estate is, I'm told, a great thing to have in your portfolio. So I'm doing this thing. I'm terrified. I could lose a lot.

But the alternative is to *stand still*, and I won't do that. I did once. I won't anymore.

You ARE Worthy

So we've come to the end of this short part of the book, and before you read on, I want you to look inside yourself and honestly answer one question:

Am I worthy of being a Master to someone else?

If the answer isn't a firm, resounding "yes," then go back and re-read this Part of the book. You *are* worthy, and until you realize that, until you realize that the worth of a Master is in their apprentices, then you're holding yourself back.

Part III: Achieve Your Success

What does "success" mean? YOU get to decide. Just you. And once you've decided what it is, you'll find that it's actually not really that complex to achieve it. This Part of the book is entirely new for this 4th Edition, and it represents a subtle, yet critical, change in how I've been coaching people through achieving their success.

Define Your Self

I deliberately used "Your Self" in the title of this chapter instead of "Yourself." That's because, in this chapter, I want you to think about your *self*. Who you *are*, at your core. What your values are; what you care about. Who you want to *be*.

I want—and I realize this is a little morbid—you to write your obituary. A long-form one. Don't worry about the "...is survived by their loving spouse and two children" part; you don't need to make this *that* morbid. No, instead, focus on the *kind of life you led before you died.*

I'll give you an example.

 Don was a well-known technology instructor, and helped thousands of people learn new technologies that positively impacted their careers and their lives. He evolved into a reliable business leader, and played an important role in his companies' success.
Don was also concerned about people's ability to live their best life. He's known for having inspired at least a few people to examine their lives closely, and to make decisions that took them down their best path.
Don was known for his generosity with his friends and others around him. His family led an enjoyable life, filled with friends, vacations to the places they loved, and a stable home. There was always food on the table, and while Don and his family didn't have everything, they wanted for nothing.
Don was also known for his charitable work, including the founding of a nonprofit dedicated to technology education that exists still. His contributions supported education, feeding the needy, children' advocacy, and the performing arts.

That's *my* Self. That's who I want to have been when I die. I'm living many of those things now, but not all of them, which means I still have some living to do. But those are the things I want other people to look back at my life and say about it. Note that some of those things related to my personal life, while others relate to my profession; together, these are my *life*.

These aren't goals. I haven't specified how many people I want to teach, how much money I want to have given over my life, or the specific destinations I want to take my family to. My definition of self isn't necessarily something you can measure, nor is it entirely a list you can just check things off of. For example, if I took a vacation to Pigeon Forge to go to Dollywood, does that check off the "vacations to places the loved?" It might contribute to it, and it might not. Reading it, you wouldn't know if I actually enjoyed Dollywood or if it was a family trip I swore I'd never repeat.

Goals, on the other hand, *should* be measurable. If I had written a goal, like, "visit Aruba every other year," an external observer could look at my behavior and tell if I'd met the goal or not.

Your definition of self is *not* a list of goals. It is a retrospective description of your life, and it's useful because you're writing it *before you die*.

Your definition of self also doesn't need to be terribly specific. I haven't mentioned what I taught people, merely that I did. Keep it high-level and aspirational. Focus on the things *that are important to you, personally*. The things *you* care about. Think about what you really, really, truly, most care about in life, and make sure those things are all represented in this definition.

Some examples of other good statements I've seen:

- "...always made it to the kids' soccer games."
- "...became a prominent leader in her field."
- "...saw both of his kids through college."
- "...lived near and was loved by a large extended family."

Those are the kinds of aspirational statements I'm looking for.

 Do it. Start thinking about what's important to you. I started by making an informal bullet list, and you can actually stop there if you want. I'm a writer, so obviously turning that list into something more prose-like was inevitable.

As I'm writing this, I'm hoping that you make *helping others* a part of your definition, and I'm especially hoping you make *teaching others* part of it. But you don't need to; that's just my bias, and my belief that our lives are measured by the lives we've helped, and nothing else. You are perfectly allowed to feel differently, and craft your definition accordingly.

This is actually a good time to think, in *broad* terms, about who you might want to help or teach, and how you might want to help or what you might want to teach. I shared a couple of things I wanted to be known for teaching—again, no hard specifics, but enough to get the gist. My statement isn't who I *am,* but it's who I'm striving to *be.*

I actually suggest you spend some time on this before you continue reading.

Know Yourself

OK, if "Define Your Self" is about stating who you want to be, then you need to take a step back and figure out *who you are*. Here's why: if who you want to be is point B, then who you presently are is point A, and we need to construct a path between those two. But knowing yourself isn't about writing an aspirational statement. We don't need to *aspire* to be who we are; we already *are*, right? So we just need to document it a little.

What are your strengths, and what are your weaknesses? Acknowledging both is really important, because we need to know what tools we've got to work with, and we need to know what barriers might been the way. And this isn't saying you need to make a New Year's resolution to fix all of your weaknesses! We all have weaknesses, and we might *like* some of them, or simply be unwilling to do what's necessary to change them. That's fine, but we still have to at least acknowledge them.

STRENGTHS
I write quickly.
I am very focused on meeting deadlines that I agree
to.
I can be personable when I want to be.
I can be authoritative when I want to be.
I write like a speak. I use everyday language that is
not opaque or filled with business-isms.
I can be counted on to be my word.

WEAKNESSES
I am very risk-averse.
I am uncomfortable changing my routines.
I struggle to work on teams, especially in person.
I am an introvert.
I can be overly firm in sharing my opinions.
I am pretty sarcastic.

Note that weaknesses and strengths aren't absolutes. Being risk-averse *can* be a weakness, and it's one I've struggled with over the years, but that doesn't mean I want to become completely risk-accepting, either. Everything is a spectrum, and I just feel I'm a little further in one direction than might be healthy for me—but try as I might, I can't fix it. I'm kind of at a point where I've done as much as I feel I can, and I'm just going to have to work within the parameters of how my brain happens to be.

Writing quickly is a strength, and it's one I've relied heavily on for much of my career. But it's not a categorically Good Thing; I make my share of typos that a more deliberate typist might not make, which makes me a heavier edit at times, and often results in the odd tpyo making it through to a final manuscript.

With all that written down, I've got some thinking to do. Flip back to my definition of self—what do you see in my strengths and weaknesses that might help me, or slow me down, in getting to where I want to go? It's an important question, because I may need to decide that I either need to correct a weakness, or drop something from my definition. For example, if I felt I was notoriously tight-fisted with money, that might not be compatible with the charitable giving I aspire to. Or, if I wanted to succeed as a writer, knowing that I'm strong at writing quickly might reinforce the possibility of that coming true. Or, if my introversion was going to make it harder for me to be an effective business leader, I might decide that working on my introversion would be a worthy thing to undertake, so that I could eventually be the self I aspire to.

 Give it some thought. What strengths do you have that will support your definition of self, and what weaknesses might stand in the way? Is there anything that you might need to drop from your self definition, or is there something that one of your strengths might prompt you to add? Are any of your weaknesses things you feel you want to work out, so that they don't stand in your way?

It's probably a good idea to get this exercise done before you keep reading, because the next bit is very dependent on this.

Define "Success"

Now that you know who you want to be, what needs to happen in your professional life to make it happen?

As a quick review, here's my example definition of self, along with some commentary about how it intersects with my professional life.

> Don was a well-known technology instructor, and helped thousands of people learn new technologies that positively impacted their careers and their lives. He evolved into a reliable business leader, and played an important role in his companies' success.

This is a pretty clear connection to my professional life. I may need to add some business skills and leadership skills that I don't currently possess, which might mean making the time for that learning to happen. It might even mean I need to earn enough money to take some classes. That's important to recognize, along with the fact that such learning might take time that I need to account for.

> Don was also concerned about people's ability to live their best life. He's known for having inspired at least a few people to examine their lives closely, and to make decisions that took them down their best path.

This starts to drift between personal and professional life. If I want books like this one to be able to help people, I need to find a way to get the word out, and right now my audience is predominantly tech people from a specific area of tech. I can ask for their help, but I may need to hire someone who's good at marketing for their expertise.

That'll cost money, which I need to factor it—I need to be earning enough to pay for that, for example.

> Don was known for his generosity with his friends and others around him. His family led an enjoyable life, filled with friends, vacations to the places they loved, and a stable home. There was always food on the table, and while Don and his family didn't have everything, they wanted for nothing.

There are some pretty clear financial implications in this bit, and it's where I'd need to sit down and really come up with a salary number that enables all this. In fact, this exact kind of statement is where most people get into the "rat race" really hardcore, jumping from job to job or position to position, in search of every-more money and every-higher titles. That's because they're just focusing on *more,* without really knowing what they *need* to support the life they want. They're living to work, not working to live.

With a good definition of self, and some numbers to reveal how that self can come to be, you can exit the rat race entirely, and pursue what you *need* and *want* in a very focused, deliberate, and thoughtful fashion.

> Don was also known for his charitable work, including the founding of a nonprofit dedicated to technology education that exists still. His contributions supported education, feeding the needy, children' advocacy, and the performing arts.

Again, some financial stuff here, which I need to take into account. Then I can define my *success.* In other words, in my professional life, what does *success* look like?

As with your definition of self, *avoid writing down milestones.* Instead, look back at your entire career and tell me what it looked like, in broad strokes. There *will* probably be some overlap with your definition of self: for many of us, our professions *are* a huge part of our selves. That's fine. But try and keep your personal life out of your professional life, to the degree you're able to. Focus on success being a description of your career. And remember: *your career is a means to an end.* Your career is something you do to *get the life you aspire to.* So whatever you state in your definition of success, it should directly support your life aspirations.

 I will be known as an author who produces helpful, entertaining, informative, and valuable works of fiction and nonfiction. I will write pieces that I enjoy writing, and I will also write pieces that earn money, and I recognize that those two are not always going to be the same.

I will be known as a capable business leader who can lead a team toward a company's vision. I will retire from a position of senior leadership.

I will earn at least $150,000[^This is an entirely made-up number, because I feel it's important you put an actual number and not a vague statement.] before taxes each year. I am stating that in 2020 dollars in the United States of America, and I will adjust that number annually to account for inflation and other factors outside my control.

I will work in a field, and for an organization, that provides me ample time for family vacations and other personal time—at least four weeks annually.

Hopefully, you get the idea. Now, these won't all happen at once, and for the most part I'm not putting a timeline on them. This is what my success looks like, not a statement for when I'll get there.

It is fine to adjust your success definition when you need to. I re-examine mine annually. More often, I feel, is just moving the target too much and renders all my efforts too unstable, but annually is a chance to revisit my choices and thoughts. My actual success definition—which I've been working on since 2002—is much longer and more refined than the above example, but it also gets into a pretty personal level of specificity that wouldn't necessarily be helpful to you.

De-Conflict

Now it's time to de-conflict. That is, you need to put your self definition and success definition side-by-side and see where they conflict.
For example, what if, for your self, you'd written something like:

 ...is a person who always made it to the kids' games
and other activities, and was known as a loving parent
who was always present.

But for your success definition, you wrote:

 I will work for a large international firm that afford
me with both reach and opportunity, and which grants
me frequent opportunities for international travel.

Those two aren't in sync. You're going to need to modify something.
Or, what if for your self, you'd written something like:

 ...provided a large and luxurious home for his family,
and enjoyed treating them to vacations in exotic
places, where his children learned to be citizens of the
world.

A worthy goal, but what if it was paired with a success definition
that included:

 I will work for a small, closely-held firm, and will need
less than $100,000 per year in before-tax salary.

That might not be compatible (although it might be where you plan to live, I dunno), and it's definitely something you must de-conflict before proceeding.

We've all seen those movies where the father gets so wrapped up in business that he ignores his kids, and is missing them growing up[^If you haven't I recommend *Hook* or *Mary Poppins*.], is barely saved, and finally quits his overbearing job and learns to live on less so that he can enjoy his children's lives. Defining your self, then defining your success, and then de-conflicting the two, is how you avoid that happening.

- Your Self is who you want to be.
- Your Success is *only those things* which enable your Self to come into being.

Process all of the conflicts between the two. Decide what's possible, and aim for it. You'll need to do this before moving on to the next steps, where you start to craft an actual plan to put this all into action.

 Go ahead: de-conflict your Self and Success until the two can live in harmony with each other, with your Success directly supporting who you want your Self to be.

In the next couple of chapters, I'm going to insert some context and caveats, before we proceed to working on your actual plan toward success. If reading the next two chapters makes you change your mind about anything in your Self or Success, by all means come back and work on them some more.

Laziness and Discipline

Laziness is built into the human body. I had a personal trainer at the gym once, and he constantly struggled in getting me to lift weights with the correct form. Oh, I wasn't so bad that I was in risk of hurting myself—I understand form for safety's sake—but I'd just let my body take little shortcuts that *made it easier.* He'd point it out, and I'd point out that, well, *it was easier* my way. Engineers always try to find the most efficient route, right? He pointed out that *easier* wasn't really the point of the gym, and that I was cheating myself.

That made me think.

Laziness is cheating yourself.

Do you know another reason why we're often lazy? We, as human beings, cannot easily contemplate our own mortality (this isn't always the root cause of laziness but it's often related). That's generally a good thing; if we went around worrying about dying all the time, we'd likely get nothing done. But it means we also have difficulty contemplating the future in concrete, chronological terms. It's a vague cloud to us, most of the time. We've all the time in the world, so there'll be plenty of time to do whatever.

But there won't. I mean, first, you *will die.* We've ample evidence backing that up. But even short of full brain death, there *isn't* always time. Something else will come up. Procrastination is an evil loop. It's like a payday loan that you can't pay off and have to roll over, and over, and over. You end up barely paying the interest and never making headway on getting anything done.

Don't be lazy. If you *can* do something today, right now, then just *do it* (turns out Nike had it right all along). And don't just half-ass it so that you can check it off your list. If something is worth doing, do it well and do it right. And do it *now.*

Think about it: You could goof off and do it—whatever "it" is—later. But when later comes along, you may be faced with two situations. First, something else might have come up, and so "it" will get pushed even further down the track. Second, you finally buckle down to do "it," and end up missing out on some great opportunity.

Writing a book. Reading a book. Writing a blog article. Updating your resume. *Sending* out that resume. Mentoring that kid. Taking that class. Getting that degree. These are all things we push off every day, when they're the things that should matter the most. They're the things that are worth the time, in both the short and the long run. And if you're truly looking to become the Master and begin passing on your craft ... there's no time like the present.

You'll have plenty of time to relax and goof off—and if you don't, you'll still have accomplished amazing things. But amazing things don't accomplish themselves. Good things do *not* come to those who wait. Good things come to those who *do*, and who do it *now*. Seize not only the day but **every** day of your entire life.

The *easiest* thing to do... is nothing.

So I'll contrast that with the hard thing: discipline.

Discipline is nothing more than *remembering why you started a thing in the first place*. Why that thing was valuable, and why it's something you wrote down in your to-do list. This is why defining your success, defining your self, and writing down those definitions is *so incredibly important*. They're your reminders. *They* are why you are doing the things you're doing, and their value should be clear to you. Anytime you start to waver, or feel like you're going to fall off the wagon, get your The Grind workbook back out, and re-read your success and self definitions. These are things *you said were important to you*. Are they still? If not, perhaps they need to be rewritten.

I'll give you an example, and it's in the gym again.

When I started with my most recent trainer, he naturally asked what my fitness goals were. I told him—absolutely straight-faced and deadpan—that I intended to pursue a late-life career as an underwear model. I waited about a minute for him to find a polite way to explain to me that I was aiming too high, and then laughed, and said, "kidding."

But we did talk about my goals, and my diet, and my level of commitment. And we learned that I was unwilling to give up my evening wine or whiskey. "That'll slow you down," he said. I thought about it, and I answered, "I know. I'm fine with it." And that night, I went home and adjusted my current The Grind workbook. I *wanted* to be lazy about a moderate level of alcohol consumption. And there was no point in fighting it, because I didn't want to. And so I adjusted my plan for it.

Laziness and discipline are part of who we are. You need to decide when you're going to address it, and if you *choose* not to, you need to decide what that will prevent you from having. Just be honest with yourself about it.

Look Around... But Look Closely

A danger inherent in modeling your life or career, even in part, on someone else is that you tend to see only that person's "end state." You see where they are *now*, but you don't necessarily see how they got there. You don't see whatever hard times they may have encountered, the mistakes they may have made, or the sacrifices they may have made. It's easy to *want to be successful;* it's something else entirely to *become* that way.

When possible, try to get to know the exemplars in your life. Ask them questions—do they have any regrets about where they are now? Was there anything notable they had to do to get there? Where was the hard work, and what might you have to prepare yourself for if you want to follow even partway in their footsteps?

Drawing from others' experiences is wonderful—being the apprentice to their Master, if you will. But you have to make sure to *fully* draw from their experiences. Don't just look at the high notes and the outcomes; teaching is, ultimately, a way for someone to share their *mistakes* with you so that you can perhaps avoid those same mistakes. But when it comes to something as personal as your career and life, not many of us are willing to share those mistakes. They're embarrassing, after all. And so we put on a good face for the world, and hide the hard times and low notes. Try to push past that, if you can, or at least spend some serious time imagining those mistakes so that you can get a fuller picture.

And at the end of the day, don't be too surprised if someone you admire says that their main secret to success is mainly "hard work." Try to dig into what that means, with as much specificity as possible. For example, I have a friend who, he will tell you, definitely works hard. He gets to work at around 10 each day, takes an hour for lunch, usually plays foosball in the office for half an hour or so, kids around with his co-workers throughout the day, and leaves at 4. Who am I to say that's not "hard work?" For *me*, it isn't, and it isn't the kind of workday that got me to the place I wanted to be, but for *him,* it's a solid day, and it's gotten him to where *he's* comfortable in life. "Hard work" is always a good answer to "how do I get further in my life?" but there's a lot of detail behind those two words that you want to try to ferret out.

Looking around you should *not* be a way to define your goals. It should be a way to find other people who've already achieved your goals from whom you can maybe crib a tip or two in building your own plan to get there. So as you complete this step, start making notes about your plan.

Now, for an important caveat.

One thing I've noticed about a lot of people is that they'd love to *have done something,* but they're less interested in *doing* that something. Many people like to *be successful,* but they're not always aware of, or interested in, the work that it takes to get there. We look around and see what others have, or what others achieve, and we want what they've got and what they've done. That's actually not a terrible thing–it's what role models are for!

The thing is, the *journey* is actually the important bit, not the destination. Life is worth living because of the journey, because at the end—well, there's only the end. Successful people are successful because they made the journey. They made the mistakes along the way. They took risks, and some paid off and others didn't. Indeed, most people you'd probably regard as successful likely don't consider themselves all that successful–they're still on the journey, and probably will be for most of their lives.

Having something is less important than *getting* something. That's why we can all serve as Masters for someone else, but should still be very much apprentices and journeymen ourselves. Knowing that "you're not there, yet" doesn't stop you from helping someone else, teaching them, and guiding them, because *none* of us should be "there" yet. Because the journey, the attempt, and the effort is what's really worth it, we should all constantly be on that journey, making that attempt, and expending that effort; none of that means we should stop looking behind us to see who else is on the road.

 Timothy hadn't worked at the smithy for a week when he was already tired of all the sweeping and scut-work. "When will I get to do the easy stuff like you?" he asked his Master.

"Oh, ho, you think this is the easy stuff," his Master chuckled. "You see the scars on my arms? Those were from hot steel, poured too fast. You see this finger, shorter then it should be? A hammer on the anvil, swung wrong. And you see that new window in the wall? An expensive replacement after the men I borrowed money from smashed its predecessor. You've much road to walk down before you'll arrive at where I am today."

Make a Plan, and Get Permission

OK - you should know what "success" means to you. You should have a strong definition for the kind of person you want to be in work and in life. You should have some ideas about how others have gotten to a similar point. You should have started mentally doing a "gap analysis" between where you are right now and where you want to be. You should have started to formulate a plan, perhaps to take the first couple of steps along the way.

Stop.

In all likelihood, you're not the only person in your life. Whatever you're planning is going to need to involve your loved ones—boyfriend, wife, kids, dog, whatever. They may have to sacrifice along with you so that the entire "team" can benefit in the end. They might have to be okay with you coming home late, traveling more, missing school recitals, or being away on a birthday or anniversary. *Get their permission* up front. The people in your life—even your closest friends—are your partners in life, or should be, and they should have some input into that partnership.

If you take this step, you may find yourself with some good advice to help shape your plan. You may find yourself with the moral support you need to start making those first steps. You may, of course, get some pushback, too—and you'll need to decide if you want to adjust your plan accordingly.

With the collaboration of the important people (or dogs) in your life, start fleshing out the first steps of your new life plan. Make sure they understand your definition of success and how you've defined who you want to be. And if your goal is indeed to become a Master - to eventually be able to help others along in *their* careers or lives—make that clear, too. Ask for help in crafting a plan that brings you your success and places you in a position where you're able to help those coming up behind you.

It's also important to put some timelines and metrics on your plan. For me, it was, within 18 months, having written a certain number of books, spoken at a certain number of conferences, and gotten a regular column in a trade publication. Those were outcomes I could easily look at and objectively measure.

 If you're going to use The Grind, this is the perfect time to flip to your first Monthly Plan and write down your actual Plan. Keep it actionable, and make notes of the objective, observable outcomes you'll use to measure your progress. Remember, your Plan can and will evolve over time, so this is just the first in an ever-changing series of drafts.

This is where *milestones* come into play.

Defining Milestones

Let me reiterate a couple of key points:

- Define Your Self is where you decide the kind of life you want to have lived when you die.
- Know Yourself is knowing the strengths and weaknesses that will contribute to, or stop you from, getting the life you want.
- Define Your Success is how you decide what will be needed to get the life you want. This is kind of an "end state" description, sort of your penultimate life goal. By definition, once you hit your success, you're "done" and you can enjoy your life.

So getting from where you are now, to where your success is, requires a plan, and you're going to build that plan in the form of milestones.

Milestones are:

- Things that you need to achieve in order to get to your success.
- Things that any external observer can see if you've achieved or not. That is, these aren't internalized things; they're concrete things that can be measured.
- Things that have dates attached to them. These should be reasonable dates, based on some basic research that you've conducted.
- Things that you can *see* being done. Critically, you don't need to map out every milestones between now and your eventual success; only map out as far as you can see and understand. The rest will come later.

Milestones are the things you actually work toward on your monthly and weekly plans. They're the prizes. They're the goals. Milestones are important because they're usually fairly close-in—don't define milestones that will require more than two years to achieve; instead, break them down as needed. Humans don't focus well on ten-year destinations, but we can do really well in shorter timeframes. But because your milestones *create a path to your success,* you can rest easy that, if you work toward those shorter-term goals, the long-term success will happen.

Example

Let me start by revisiting my definition of success. Let's presume for the sake of discussion that it's 100% compatible with my definition of self, and that I've totally de-conflicted it. Since I tossed a salary number into that success, let's assume, again for the sake of argument, that I'm presently making $120,000 a year, $30,000 short of my stated need. I'll insert commentary in the form of the milestones I might choose to define for my next few years. I'll also insert some of the "side notes" I might make to myself—tasks I want to undertake, but which aren't necessarily connected to the solid, measurable outcomes of a milestone.

> I will be known as an author who produces helpful, entertaining, informative, and valuable works of fiction and nonfiction. I will write pieces that I enjoy writing, and I will also write pieces that earn money, and I recognize that those two are not always going to be the same.

Milestones:

- By the end of 2020, complete two fiction trilogies.
- By the end of 2020, have an audience marketing reach of at least 2,000.
- By the end of 2022, complete a third trilogy, along with two "fun" pieces not intended to generate revenue.
- By the end of 2022, have at least 20 Amazon review for each of my published books, and an audience marketing reach of at least 10,000.

See how these are measurable, objective outcomes that support the more high-level and aspirational success definition? These are "how I get there." If the definition is the goal, then these are the waypoints along the way. At least I *think* they are; time will tell if I'm right, something we address in the next chapter.

> I will be known as a capable business leader who can lead a team toward a company's vision. I will retire from a position of senior leadership.

Milestones:

- Complete leadership training course in 2020.
- By the end of 2021, move into a team lead role within my current company, or take a new position elsewhere.
- By the end of 2021, find a mentor who can help me improve my leadership skills.
- By the end of 2022, move into a mid-management role.
- By the end of 2024-2025, move into a senior leadership role.

These milestones aren't as fully fleshed out, because I don't yet know what I might need to add to my skill set to make them happen. The point of writing them down is to force some research. I'll "Look Around," and maybe talk to people in the kind of position I'm after to see what they feel I'm missing. I've actually made *that* a milestone.

 I will earn at least $150,000 before taxes each year. I am stating that in 2020 dollars in the United States of America, and I will adjust that number annually to account for inflation and other factors outside my control.

Milestones:

- This year, look at job listings in the range I need, as well as just below, and see what I'm missing to hold down those jobs.
- By mid-2020, formulate an action plan to increase my skill set to the point where I could hold down a next-step job, preferably a team lead position in my current company.

 I will work in a field, and for an organization, that provides me ample time for family vacations and other personal time—at least four weeks annually.

Milestones:

- By mid-2020, develop a feeling for what kinds of positions or companies afford this. More tech companies are offering unlimited paid time off; investigate jobs in those companies as a primary target for future positions.

As you can see, some of these are *very* short-term milestones, and that's fine. As I reach them, which may take longer than I initially estimate, I'll develop new milestones. That's why I have a new The Grind workbook *every year:* so that I can review what I've done, and set up the next steps.

All the way, I'm making sure these goals align to my success definition, and I'm annually reviewing to ensure my success is still directly and exclusively supporting my definition of self. My "self" is where I'm going; my "success" is how I get there, and my milestones are the stops along the way.

Execute, Study, Adjust

With your plan in hand, it's time to start executing it, and more importantly, tracking your progress. That's because few plans survive first contact with the world—you're going to have to continually analyze your progress and adjust.

For me, I was having a tough time getting a magazine column that was on a topic I wanted. I had to decide which I wanted more—a column in my specified timeframe or a column *on a specific topic*. Halfway into my first 18 months, I had some heartfelt talks with the family, and we decided that having my name out there on a regular basis was more important, right then, than having my name attached to a specific topic that I wanted to be known for. *That* meant pushing back some other parts of my life plan, which involved being known *for a specific topic*. Doing both—getting my name out there *and* having it attached to that topic—was proving impractical to accomplish in a single step, so we had to change the plan.

Plans change—or they should. You need to react to the facts on the ground, not just slavishly pursue a plan that isn't playing out. I'm not saying you need to *abandon* your plan—just bear in mind that **the plan is a means to an end, not the end itself.** If the plan isn't getting you closer to your success and your life definition, then it isn't working, and you need to adjust.

Remember: the plan is just a set of milestones. If you realize that the milestones aren't pointing toward your success like you thought they would, *change them.*

This step is why The Grind has you review your Plan each month and make adjustments as needed. Maybe you're aiming too high too fast, or maybe you've changed your mind about your success. All that's fine - the Plan, like life, is meant to evolve.

Find Your Audience

Bear in mind that my goal was to achieve Mastery—to be able to *teach* people. I wanted to help people along in their careers. The first time I had an opportunity to truly teach was one of the proudest moments of my entire life, and remains so to this day. I was helping laid-off airplane mechanics re-skill into information technology, teaching night classes at a local university.

But I screwed up. As I progressed past that first step, I didn't *define my audience*. I didn't decide, specifically, *who* I wanted to help and *what* I wanted to help them do. As a result, much of my early career did a lot to get my name out into the world, but did so in a scattershot fashion. I wrote about whatever interested me, or whatever I thought would pay well at the time. In some cases, as I've mentioned, those were deliberate decisions—hey, you gotta pay the bills—but in more cases than I'd like to recall, it was just me bouncing randomly around to whatever seemed fun. You see, in my plan, I'd never really thought about *who I'd be known as*.

The turning point in my career was a Microsoft technology called VBScript. It was, essentially, a lightweight programming language designed for the people who run servers and networks for a living. VBScript could do a lot of other things, but that was a big part of its purpose—and *nobody* was really teaching it at the time. Tons of systems administrators and network engineers were struggling to use this technology and nobody was helping. So I wrote a book, in 2003, on using VBScript. It was probably my eighth or ninth book—and it changed my career. My *name* had been out there a bit, but now I was *known*. The book sold thousands and thousands of copies (rare for a tech book). I got a dozen speaking invitations a year. I started teaching my own on-site classes around the world. I recorded and sold a series of instructional videos. I wrote another book, and co-authored a handful of others with colleagues. I was helping people change their lives—students and readers would regularly tell me that mastering VBScript had gotten them a promotion, or more often, let them snag a better-paying and more-interesting job. I'd defined my audience and moved to focus almost exclusively on them—and it worked for everyone.

Technology changes, of course, and VBScript gave way to a product called PowerShell. As I write this, it's what I'm known for best, having worked with it for over a decade. But it's that same audience I started with—they're my people. Many of the folks who've read my work or seen me speak at a conference have become great friends. We're a community together, and they're the very best in the world at listening to my message of "help other people." As the technology has enabled their own career successes, they've become increasingly generous with their time, answering others' questions online, writing online tutorials, teaching their own classes, and more. Finding my audience—which was very much an active decision, back in the VBScript days, that my family and I talked about and made—helped bring me to where I am now.

That's what it's all about—or what it *should* be all about.

 The Grind includes a place to explicitly write about who you think your apprentices are. This should be a constant exercise, as you think of new things you could teach and who might benefit from them. Constantly look for new audiences who might need you.

Now that you have your audience in mind, it's time to start helping them.

Part IV: Help Others

You've realized that you're worthy. You've created a path to your success. Now it's time to put it into action, and to start helping other people do the same.

The Value of Helping

This feels like a bit of a weird chapter, right? "The value of helping?" I mean, we all know the value of helping. We all *want* to help, if we can. Helping someone is value in and of itself, right?

Well, sure. But it's not a specific value. "Value of helping someone" is a lot like "success" and "worth;" sure, they have a meaning, but it's not a concrete meaning. It's a subjective meaning, one that different people experience differently. And I feel that, a lot of times things with non-concrete, non-specific value are easier to put off. Helping someone is *vaguely* a Good Thing To Do, but *not* helping someone doesn't really diminish your own life, so it's easy to put it off.

Just like your "worth" as a Master, the value of helping someone is defined by the person being helped. If you're serving as a Master to an apprentice, it's the *apprentice* who decides what value they're taking away from the relationship. They may place more value on your help than you do, in fact. Sometimes, as with many schoolteachers, you'll never know how much value someone took away from you helping them. But you need to be deeply convinced that *value did indeed exist,* and that it's a good use of your time and energy to keep doing it.

If it helps, you can also think about helping other people as a way of paying back the significant debt you owe. You– wait, you don't owe a significant debt?

Oh, but you do.

Whatever success you've found in life, you didn't achieve that entirely on your own. "Entirely on your own" would mean you popped out of the womb, and with no further assistance from anyone, ever, you got to where you are today. Nobody assisted you, taught you, corrected you, or anything else. Of course, none of us are like that. We've *all* had help, almost continuously, and almost our entire lives. Much of that help came in small, unacknowledged ways—the friend who shared their lunch with you in school, the teacher who took an extra minute with you in class, the boss who explained how a particular part of the company worked.

Whoever you are today is, in part, due to the people who have been around you. The ones who've helped you, yes, and the ones who've hurt you or merely stood by. But the ones that helped you created a debt. Most of them didn't get anything of value from you in return. Sure, a public school teacher gets paid, and the citizens pay the taxes that pays the salary, but what did *they* get out of educating you? In the end, you've got a debt over your head, and helping others— paying it *forward,* rather than back to the people who helped you— is how you pay it off.

Look around you. Look around yourself at home, at work, at the gym, in class, or wherever you happen to be. Force yourself to see the people who could benefit a bit from something you already know how to do. Maybe it's some of the young women who go to your kids' school—what do *you* know that might be of value to *them?* What kind of person will they be if you inject some positive experiences into their lives, right now, versus if you don't?

For example, I have a friend who decided to go to his kids' school and teach the teenagers there how to change the tire on a car. He got a bunch of people to volunteer to take their cars to the school, so the kids would have several to practice on. He worked with the school, and several teachers volunteered to help out. Any teen in the school was allowed to come, but my friend did it mainly for the girls. See, *he* has two teenage girls (God bless him). He also has a wife, and his wife got a flat tire one time on her hour-long commute from home. In the winter, when it was dark. And snowing. And in an area with poor cell coverage. His wife wasn't a weakling by any stretch, and she got right to work changing the tire. But when she got home, they sat that night and she talked about how *scared* she'd been at first. How she had to remind herself that *she could do this,* and get out there and do it. And how much less dependent she felt after it was done. He decided he not only wanted his own girls to feel that way, but *all* the girls. The girls in the school might not value that help a lot at first, but they definitely will in time.

I've another reader who, like me, works in technology. But she found her apprentice audience outside her workplace. Her son is mildly autistic and nonverbal, and has some severe food allergies. She and her husband had pretty much committed to being homebodies, since taking their son out is such a chore, let alone traveling anywhere with him. But she eventually began to feel that they were robbing their son of a broader experience. They *wanted* him to see the world, or as much of it as he could. They wanted him to have experiences that he could enjoy. And so they started doing research, and made it happen. A couple of years later, she was talking to another parent in their neighborhood who was in the same situation. She realized that there was no need for every parent to have to repeat the same research and mistakes she'd made; as she learned in *Be the Master,* teaching is mainly the process of relating your past mistakes so that other people don't have to make them. So she started a class, and before long had a group of a dozen other parents of autistic kids. She kicked off the learning by sharing what she'd found and done, including her mistakes. Before long, the other parents were sharing right back. She was a Master, because as you'll learn later in this book, *Masters unite.* She brought together a group—many of them willing to be Masters as well—and they developed processes, procedures, and practices that served their "trade" of caring for their children. What "value" do you think applies to that story? Can it even be measured?

People don't always realize how much inherent value they possess. Take my field of technology: it's one of the few fields in the world that doesn't universally *demand* a four-year college degree. It's a field that exists virtually everywhere in the world. It's a field that routinely pays above-average for whatever area its practitioners live in. And it's a field that's broadly open to outsourcing and remote workers, reducing geographical barriers to finding work. If you can help someone in an underprivileged position unlock technology skills, *you have helped them unlock a new life.* Whether you're teaching them how to code up a mobile app, or teaching them to build a wireless network, or teaching them how to help someone else get their laptop working correctly—you have given that person *immense* value. Those skills can be the start of them lifting themselves up, and making a life for themselves. The "value" in that is almost limitless.

Imagine if *everyone* did that, all the time. If *everyone* said, "You know what, I'm going to *make time for this.* This is important for me to do, and I'm *going to do it.* I'm not going to put it off. I'm going to make helping other people, in the ways I can, part of my definition of my self. I will structure my career to help make the room for that. I will *do this.*"

What kind of world would that be?

Humble Helping

I've gotten into a lot of conversations with people who don't think they know anything "worth" teaching to someone. Part of that is my fault, because I started this book with the story of Timothy the Blacksmith. That kind of locks the idea of Mastery into a work setting, which is obviously where the Master/apprentice relationship started.

But remember this: a Master is *anyone who teaches*. A Master is someone who shares skills and knowledge alongside their apprentices. *Anything* you are capable of teaching, to someone who doesn't already know it, **is worthy**.

Call it "humble helping:" teaching someone how to change the tire on their car, or to change the oil. Teaching someone how to cook a healthy meal. Teaching someone how to do their taxes. Teaching someone how credit works, and helping them understand their current credit situation. Teaching someone how to change a bathroom faucet. These are small things that many of us know how to do, but that many other people *don't*. Learning these things can make someone more independent, and more in control of their own lives. That will doubtless help move them closer to their own definitions of self and success.

And *that* is why I know those "humble" topics are "worthy." The worth of something you teach is not something *you* can measure or define. It can only be measured by the *people who receive it from you*. Only they know the impact it will have on their lives.

I had a young friend who had in fact been struggling with a bathroom faucet. Changing a bathroom faucet isn't usually hard, although it also isn't often fun, what with the water and having to stick your head in the tight space under the sink. But there are a few tricks that can make it easier, and a tool called a "basin wrench" that's a godsend in certain situations. I'd changed most of the faucets in our house, and so I worked with my friend to change his. I shared what tips I knew, and pointed to a couple of websites that had been helpful to me in the past.

My friend was, at the time, employed in a very meaningless and dead-end job, and just being able to do something *useful* for himself was an enormous spirit-lifter. It was one of those little things that meant practically nothing to me in terms of time or other investment, but just meant the world to him. His parents hadn't been much for helping with the "adulting" side of life, and suddenly here he was, taking care of things in his own home, on his own.

Next thing I know, he's replaced another faucet *and* the sink. And he realizes he *really* liked doing it. He enjoyed working with his hands instead of sitting on a phone in front of a computer all day, and he enjoyed being able to see tangible results of his work. So he quit his job and became an apprentice plumber. The pay was a bit less at first, but he had some savings to get him through, and his family agreed to help where they could. He graduated from the program in just a few months, and was at work with a plumbing company in town, *loving* it. And so he decided to start taking night classes to get his electrician's license, and now he does plumbing *and* electrical work, two trades that don't normally go together.

And it was because someone took a minute to show him a couple of tricks for changing a faucet.

Nothing that you know is "unworthy" of being shared. You can never predict the impact teaching the right thing at the right time can have.

What Do You Know?

Part of The Grind is defining your "teaching catalog," meaning a list of things you know and can share. There's a point to this exercise, and it's important that you do it.

Most people who take a *Be the Master* workshop with me start off listing the obvious things, which are mainly things they know from their job. And that's fine: whatever your job is, you're probably decently skilled in it, and those are valid things to consider teaching to someone else. After all, the whole Master/apprentice relationship was traditionally defined in a work context, just like Timothy the blacksmith and his Master.

However, limiting your "things I can teach" to stuff from work *also limits your apprentice audience.* If you're the director of a funeral home, you might well have an apprentice working with you in that trade, but you're probably not going to find a large group of folks *outside* the trade with whom you can share that skill set.

So *dig deeper* as you think about what you know.

Can you run wiring for a computer network? That's a vanishing skill as wireless connections become faster and more reliable, but it's a skill still in-demand, and it's a skill worth preserving. Can you cook a meal? Again, not a skill everyone has, and it's a task many people are intimidated by. Can you make a really good cocktail? No reason not to share that, and your appreciation for the spirits involved, and you're likely to find people willing to take you up on your "Saturday night cocktail school" classes in your home.

What are you *personally* passionate about? What really lights up you eyes? Those are things, not just whatever you do at work, that you should consider sharing with others. Really thinking about *what* you can teach will help you find people to teach it to, and that's what Mastery is all about.

Contagious Teaching

So you dove in, you found an apprentice or two (or a hundred), and you're well along the journey of teaching, making space for them to succeed, and passing along what you know.

Don't forget to *teach them how to teach.*

One of the big things we all have to try and do for the generations that succeed us is to break down the barriers and toxicity that held *us* back. A big one that you can break down is our toxic relationship with the concept of teaching and learning.

Don't fail to make sure your apprentices know that *they're always ready to teach someone,* but they need to look for that someone first. They might not find themselves teaching *you* all that much (although they might surprise you), and even their direct peers and colleagues might not be in their apprentice audience. Help them understand how to do what you did: look around, *find* an apprentice audience, and *teach* them *something.*

Make teaching one of the keystones of their lives, as early out of the gate as you can. Make it clear that you're passing along information to them, and they're expected to pass along information—whether it's the same information or not—to others. Stress that their success is dependent partly on the successes of the people *they* help. Pronounce them "worthy" of being a Master, even as they remain apprentices and journeymen with you and others.

Make teaching *contagious.*

Part V: Aspects of Mastery

You'll find that the people in your life that you tend to look up to the most all exhibit some combination of these attributes. It's worth studying them. Remember, anyone who is a teacher is, by definition, a Master; by adopting these attributes, you'll be turning yourself into one of the best.

Masters Know the Problem

A Master knows what they're solving for.

Horseshoes came to be because horse's hooves were splitting and needed protection. Blacksmiths who make horseshoes *know* the problem that they're solving for, and they work to make shoes that specifically solve that problem. They don't embed jewels into a horseshoe because *that has nothing to do with solving the problem.*

You need to know the problem that *you* solve for in any given situation. For example, I had a friend who worked in information technology, doing little but creating new user accounts for new hires, and disabling the user accounts of employees who left the company. It was low-end work, fairly boring, and something she was looking to get out of by any means.

"What do you solve for?" I asked her.

She shrugged. "Employees need user accounts," she said. "So I make them."

"But surely almost all of that could be automated," I said. "HR is already entering that data someplace, why can't you just have a piece of software pick it up and do the repetitive work?"

Another shrug. "We just haven't," she said.

If the problem you are solving for is, "we need this repetitive task done, but we're too lazy to make the computers do it, even though that's literally why computers are a thing," then you're not actually bringing much value to the table. And *that* is why I feel it's so important to *understand the problem you are meant to be solving.*

I was at a friend's place, and he was making dinner for his two kids and his wife. He and I had talked about *Be the Master* before, and I asked him, "what problem are you solving right now?"

"If the kids don't eat, they'll die," he said, grinning.

I smiled back. "Sure, but you could have just gotten microwave dinners, right? It'd be faster."

"No," he said, shaking his head, "those things have way too much sodium. And I want the kids in here with me, watching me cook. I want them to see the food that goes into their meals, and I don't want them to think cooking is some mysterious dark art. In a year or two, they'll be big enough to help me, and I want them to *want* to."

"Then you're solving for a lot more than just feeding your kids," I said.

He was quiet for a minute, and then he nodded. "Yeah, I am."

He realized that he was solving for a *much* bigger, and far more valuable problem. And once he realized that, he started to solve for it more *completely*. It *wasn't* just about feeding his kids. It was also about helping them learn to make healthier choices, and helping them eventually become more self-sufficient. And so he started going over the evening's recipe with the kids before he started, and even though they were young, he'd have them gather up all the ingredients before he started. Once he fully acknowledged the scope of the problem, he was able to solve for it in an even bigger and better way.

True Masters understand what they solve for. They take the time to understand the *complete* problem, right from first principles. They craft a solution tailor-made for that *entire* problem, and they make sure their apprentices learn to do the same.

Masters Plan to Fail

One of my high school teachers was probably the first real Master I ever encountered. I was with him for half of every day for my last two years of school, learning electronics and computer repair. One time, I'd rigged up a fairly elaborate high-voltage circuit, and was ready to test it. His standing instructions were that he wanted to check our work before we energized the circuit, and so I called him over. "You're happy with it?" he asked, and I remember nodding with a pretty high level of confidence. "Okay," he said, stepping behind me. "Power on." I flipped the switch. Sparks flew. Smoke poured out of a transformer, which then burst into flames. From just behind me, a blast of white fog came out of the fire extinguisher he'd been holding at the ready, out of my sight.

"What did you do wrong?" he asked.

Masters know that their apprentices are going to make mistakes. Human beings really only learn well through mistakes. Teaching can shortcut that process to a degree, but not entirely. Especially when you're dealing with something complex, people really have to make their own mistakes and learn from them. And so the best Masters make sure that they've created a safe space for that to happen. They're prepared to deal with failure as gracefully as possible, relying on their own experience to help them predict what will go wrong. They put needed safeguards in place, *but then they let their apprentices fail.* They ensure the failure becomes a teaching moment, to maximize the value of the failure in the moment.

These days, I "plan to fail" almost habitually. When I fly and have to check luggage, I always have some basic toiletries and a change of clothes in my small carry-on, which is a piece of luggage I purchased specifically for that purpose. That way, if the airline fails to reunite me with my bag, I can still go about my life. If

I'm coming home from an international trip, and my choices are a short connection time or a very long connection, I'll often just book a connection *the next day* and spend a night in the airport hotel. That way I don't have to worry about clearing customs and immigration quickly, and I don't have to lounge around the airport for half a day. I routinely just account for failure in many of my plans.

As a Master, you want to tell your apprentices where you expect failure to occur, and you lean on your experience to tell *you* where that's likely to be. But in the moment, the only reason you'd stop your apprentice from doing something *you know is wrong* is if you need to protect their physical safety. Plan for failure as much as you can, and put measures in place to mitigate actual damage, but *let the apprentice fail* whenever you can. Turn that into a teaching moment.

There's a reason smithies have traditionally had dirt floors, right?

Masters Teach

Obviously, Masters teach. They teach topics that they're personally familiar with, and they often do it whilst working alongside their apprentices. Mastery, as I've written before, is a state you've achieved when you have something about a topic that you can share. But Masters aren't the same as your common classroom teacher/trainer; true Masters don't sit in front of a group of people and talk at them. Masters, in the Master/apprenticeship sense, are *working* professionals in the topic they're sharing. Timothy's Master didn't sit him down at a desk and run through a PowerPoint deck on how to heat metal and pour it into a mold; he *showed* him, in real life, and then stood beside him as the kid tried to do it for the first time. "Those who can't do, teach" is not a quote about a true Master of a trade. Masters *can* do.

But Masters still need to know some of the "tricks of the trade" when it comes to teaching, and that means understanding just a wee, tiny bit about cognitive science, the science of "how we learn."

At the foundation of learning is memory, and our brains store memories as collections of special cells called *neurons*, which are connected by *synapses*. These collections, or networks, encode *experiences*, which is a hugely important concept. Our brains experience the world through our five senses: touch, taste, smell, sight, and hearing. When we experience new things, various neurons light up and start looking for existing neural networks to connect to. That's why a specific chemical can seem to smell like a banana or like rotten eggs; the chemicals "light up" neurons that are already connected to other sense-memories like taste. The more times we experience something, the stronger its neural network becomes, and the more likely it is to stick with us, and the easier it is to recall. The more senses that are part of a neural network, the stronger the related memories become, too. Our brains *can* also encode facts and other information as memories. Like experience-based memories, these become stronger, and are recalled more quickly, when they're connected to existing, strong neural networks in our brains.

It's easier to teach someone to change a tire by *showing* them, and then having them *do* it, then by talking about it or showing them a diagram. Doing something engages many or all of our senses, and creates an incredibly durable, easy-to-recall memory. Simply presenting us with facts, though, doesn't "stick" quite as readily, in large part because we usually engage just one sense, like sight. Remember having to memorize your multiplication tables in fourth grade or thereabouts? The constant repetition, use of flash cards, and the like, are the only ways to make non-sensory memories "stick" in younger brains. If you were just showing someone a diagram of changing a tire, you'd probably have to show them multiple times, over several days, before their brains finally gave up and accepted it.

This is one reason why Master/apprentice learning, as opposed to classroom learning, can be so much more effective for so many different topics. Apprentices are *doing* things. They're making mistakes, which triggers undesirable failure responses in their brains, making their brains hungry for the "fix," and more likely to remember that fix for a long period of time. When an apprentice encounters that same situation again, the relevant neurons "light up," and their neural network includes "here's how we screwed that up last time, and here's how not to do it again" information. Problem, solution, finished.

Take the pressure priority module in an F-14 jet. In normal conditions, this module directs hydraulic pressure from the pumps mounted in the engines to the rest of the aircraft's hydraulic actuators. However, if the pressure falls below a certain threshold, valves in the module close, reserving whatever pressure is left for the most crucial actuators that run the main flight controls. I remember all this because I pressure-tested dozens of these units as an apprentice. I don't remember the exact pressure where the cut-out happens, because I learned that in class.

The way our brains learn offers another important tip for teaching: we learn best when we can connect new information to existing information. That's because we're leveraging an existing neural network, rather than building a new one from scratch, which might require a lot of repetition and practice. It's one reason we use analogies to make a point: inaccurate as they can be in detail, analogies let us "latch on" to existing neural networks. I use automative analogies *a lot*, because most people I deal with are familiar with cars and what they do. As you're teaching an apprentice, then, it's important to carefully sequence the tasks you teach them, so that they can build on each other. I wouldn't start a new automotive mechanic on a task like pulling an engine block; that's a complex task. I'd start them on simpler things, letting them get used to the tools of the trade and some of the tricks, and gradually work up to the more complex things. Being a Master requires you to *think* about what you're teaching; you can't just run through random tasks willy-nilly, because your apprentice won't learn effectively.

"Are you ready, Timothy?" his Master asked.

"I think so," Timothy replied, standing at the forge. "We heated the metal just like we did for that pot yesterday, right?"

"Correct. And, like the pot, once the metal is hot..." he prompted.

"We pour it in the mold," Timothy said.

"Correct. But what's different about this mold?"

"It's not shaped like a knife at all."

"No, we'll get just a flat piece of steel out of it."

"But that's not a knife," Timothy observed.

"It is not," his Master replied. "And this is where more complex items differ from simpler ones. We'll need to forge this on the anvil to make it stronger and less brittle, and then we'll need to grind an edge onto it."

"So everything starts the same, but then we add more to it."

"More or less," his Master replied. "Go ahead and get the ladle and we'll get started."

A lot of people think they're on the road to "Be the Master" by doing a lunchtime lecture with their colleagues at work, or by showing someone how to accomplish a particular task. Those are certainly worthwhile pursuits, but they're not *Mastery*. Mastery means really thinking about what it is you want your apprentice to learn, and thinking about what they already know that you can build on. If the answer is "nothing," then you need to roll it back a bit and start teaching something simpler that they *can* connect to something they already know. We all learn in stages; you were taught to add before you were taught to multiply, and taught to multiply before you were taught to divide. Those operations build on each other, enabling you to use simpler ones to understand the more complex ones.

You'll also want to avoid the mistake of trying to sit down and explain everything up front. Remember, our brains learn best by *doing*. Timothy's Master didn't sit him down at a desk and *explain* how to make a knife. He put him right into the task, and then stood by and explained the exact bit that they were about to do. Then they did that bit. Then he'd explain the next bit, and they'd do that bit. You introduce new knowledge and abstract concepts *just before they're needed*, so that the brain doesn't have to "hold on" to them for very long before they become needed.

You'll want to make sure, before you teach anything to anyone, that you've made sure they understand the *problem* you're both trying to solve. There's no way Timothy could have really learned to make a proper horseshoe until he understood what a horse was, what hooves were, and how horseshoes protected hooves from damage. The horseshoe is a *solution*; understanding the *problem* is the key to making the solution. Without understanding the problem, Timothy might have made horseshoes that had the wrong shape, or were made of metal that was too soft. His Master likely brought him to a farrier's shop and showed him a horse, and let him examine its hooves. He showed him where nails could be driven and where they couldn't. He probably tried to show him a horse whose hooves had been damaged, and how a proper shoe could have prevented that. Understanding the *problem space* is what separates a problem *solver* from a trained monkey that's just going through some prescribed motions.

This is at the core of Mastery. Understanding your topic and *sharing* it with someone, not just talking to them about it. *Thinking* about how tasks build on one another, and creating *experiences* for your apprentices.

Masters Make Room

One notable thing about a true Master is that they make room for their apprentices to succeed. That is, at some point, you realize that *your* career is where you need it to be—that's actually the whole point of defining your success. Once you get close to that point, or actually hit it, it's time to start making room for *other* people to succeed.

I was, at one stage, the Director of Training and Curriculum for an in-person training company. I had about five trainers who reported to me, and it was pretty easy. They were all professional adults who didn't need "managing" as much as they just needed "coordinating," so that everyone was doing the right thing at the right time. After a bit, the president of the company asked if I'd be willing to be director over the company's software development business as well. Basically, running the entire company under him. I was all of 27 years old or something, and I very truthfully told him I'd love to, but that I didn't have the experience. I didn't know how to do some of the fundamental things that were part of the job, like managing our accounts receivable, engaging with customers, managing the lead software developers—none of it. "Well," he said, "then we'll have to teach you those things as you go."

That one decision on his part, and his absolute willingness to follow through on it, changed by career *forever*. I learned to manage a business. I learned to read a profit and loss statement. I learned the basics of bookkeeping and how to manage receivables. I learned how to negotiate with an upset customer. Those skills directly enabled me to go independent a few years later, let me eventually move into senior leadership positions when I later took a job again, and more.

The point is that he saw something in me that I didn't, and he created the space for me to learn and grow. He pushed, and asked me to stretch myself, but gave me the support I needed to not fail at it. He was every bit a Master to my apprentice, and it was profoundly important to me. It gave me a set of skills that eventually helped me realize much of my success definition, and supported the kind of life I wanted for myself and my family.

It's all about creating *space*. If there's a job you *could* do, but there's someone junior to you who could *learn* to do it, then a true Master will give that junior person the shot, work with them, and help them grow.

Some folks in the business world worry that by helping people grow like that, you run the risk of them leaving the business. And you do, but I regard it as a good thing. We're not on this earth for "the business;" we're on this earth for the people around us. I tell my employees that they're going to learn a lot from me— everything I can possibly teach them, in fact. And if they're ready to use those new skills to move up, but the company doesn't have a place for them, then I'll happily write the recommendation letter for wherever they wind up.

I *want* everyone on my team to move up in support of their own success. If that means they surpass me, or leave me, then that's absolutely fine. I delegate as much of my own tasks as possible to them, so that they can basically learn everything about *my* job.

That actually makes it easier for *me* to move around in the company. When an interesting opportunity comes up, I can confidently say that someone, if not someones, will be ready to be promoted and take over my current role. It's *easier* to move up, or move around, when you've got your replacement trained and lined up.

So look around you and see who you should be making space for. And this doesn't just happen at work: it can happen around the house, it can happen in your community groups, it can happen everywhere. It's one of the truest markers of a real Master.

Masters Protect

F-14s are a *semi monocoque* structure, meaning they have traditional structural elements like ribs and spars, but that the shell, or skin, of the aircraft also provides a lot of the overall structure. So, in various spots on the plane, the skin panels aren't just thin metal-and-whatever; they're thick, rigid honeycomb structures laminated between outer layers. Because you don't want seawater getting into some of the compartments those panels cover (remember, the F-14 was launched from aircraft carriers, which are replete with seawater), they all get sealed up. To do that, we'd make form-in-place gaskets. Basically, you coat the skin panel with a release agent, pour a bunch of goop on to the spot where the panel attached, and then attach the panel over the goop. The goop would dry, forming a perfect gasket matched to that panel's specific eccentricities, stuck to the spot where the panel fastened down. After the goop dried, you'd detach the panel, which would more or less pop off the sealant due to the release agent. The idea was to get a perfect, custom-made gasket that would last for several years of the panel being attached and detached.

Unless you forgot the release agent.

Then, you'd have a panel essentially glued to the aircraft, and you'd have to pry it off, which inevitably required you to delaminate the panel, ruining a component that cost God-knows-how-many-thousands of dollars.

Now, *I* did not do this, in part because I *loved* slopping release agent all over the place. But another apprentice *did*. And when the shop lead... and floor lead... and department head... and facility Lieutenant... and engineers... all came down to look at the mess, the mechanic that the apprentice had been working with stood right next to him and said, "it's my fault."

And in a way, it was; when you're Mastering someone, it's your job to keep an eye on them. But you also can't micro-manage, and *mistakes will happen*. They happen to everyone. As Master, it's your responsibility to *take* responsibility. Sure, maybe the apprentice will get a review of proper procedures in a grim tone of voice, but the *mistakes will happen*. It's how we learn. I guarantee that apprentice never made *that* mistake again. And management wasn't happy, but they understood; nobody got in serious trouble.

> Fun story: as civil servants, we referred to ourselves as, "old missiles, because we don't work, and we can't be fired." Your tax dollars at work.

Being a Master means accepting the blame when your apprentice screws up, and then *not* beating your apprentice into a bloody pulp using a 1-1/4" box-end wrench. It means taking a deep breath, walking through the *concepts* again to make sure the apprentice understands *why* things are done the way they are, and make sure they realize that they don't know as much as the obviously thought they did, and that it's better to take it slow and do it right than to rush through it and screw it up.

Being a Master does *not* mean never placing your apprentice into a situation where they can fail. You want to keep them from hurting themselves, but *failure is how we learn*. Being a Master does mean reviewing each task you're about to complete, to go over the why's, the how's, and the when's and where's; it means making sure you've covered safety precautions ("let's make sure the power is unplugged, yeah?"). All that is part of learning. Ask questions to make sure your apprentice "gets it." And then let them do their thing. Watch them as much as you can, especially at first, but don't be so protective that you prevent them from having the experiences that apprenticeships are all about.

Being a Master can be scary, because even if it's not your fault...
well, it is. It's why classroom teaching isn't quite the same thing;
once the students leave the classroom, the teacher isn't expected to
be responsible for them.

 "They're all too short!" the customer screamed at
Timothy's Master. "I ordered two-inch nails and your
stupid apprentice made one-inch nails! What're you
going to do about it?"

Timothy's Master hefted his heaviest hammer, re-
minding the customer that he was no pushover.
"That's not true," he said. "I made that order. I got
it wrong. We'll obviously remake it today, and bring
them over tomorrow."

The customer sputtered. "You did not," he spat. "I saw
that little whelp making them."

Timothy's Master took a step forward. "You're
wrong," he said quietly. "We'll have the new ones for
you shortly. Now, go." The customer looked at the set
of the Master's jaw, huffed, and left the smithy. The
Master sighed. "Last time you sent two-inch instead
of one-inch," he said softly.

"I'm sorry," Timothy said. "I was keeping them in
order on the shelf, but I think I mixed them up."

"And that is why we measure the mold before we cast
the nails," his Master reminded him. "Now, I want
you to measure every mold, and scratch the size onto
the top face. Maybe that'll keep this from happening
again."

Timothy nodded sadly, and went to start his new task.

Now, you might be thinking, "Well, this is no big deal. It's not like
I'm going to be running a full apprenticeship program—I'm just
sharing information with junior colleagues." You could still take it

up a level. You can still take it from "I'm going to demo a task for you" and really take it to Mastery. "I'm going to work *with* you on that," you might say, "because there are some cool tricks that'll save you time and keep you out of trouble. Now, let's make sure you know what could go wrong here, so we know what trouble we're avoiding." *That* is Mastery. Even if only for ten minutes as part of the work day, it's Mastery, and it's what I hope you'll aspire to.

Masters Learn

The *whole point* of Mastery is that Masters are *practitioners* of their trades. They're actively working in it, which means they're likely still learning.

That's important, because of our generally toxic relationship with education. Consider "Make the Most of the First Day of Class"[1] where more than half of the "eight concrete objectives" are about *the instructor,* not the students *per se.* Many adult educators are taught to establish authority up front, which means it's difficult to be exposed as someone who doesn't know everything. Many instructors are terrified of being "found out" as less-than-omniscient; the best few are upfront about their lack of Total Knowledge.

But those are classroom situations, and that's not what true Mastery is about. In a true Master/apprentice relationship, Masters can be learning new things all the time, even from their apprentices. Remember:

 ... In fact, Edmund through sheer accident discovered a technique for casting smaller parts with more precision, a technique he shared, with all the excitement of his youth, with Timothy. The two of them immediately devised a new lock design that took advantage of the new casting technique.

A true Master is not only able to admit that they are still learning, they're *excited* about it. They're *proud* of it. Look at two of our modern fields where apprenticeships are a reality in fact, if not in name: medicine and law. Both fields include extensive book learning, but they also require extensive on-the-job ~~apprenticeships~~ internships

---

[1]https://www.cmu.edu/teaching/designteach/teach/firstday.html

or residencies. And both require graduate practitioners to engage in continual learning, through industry-mandated ongoing education. Those industries recognize their own constant state of change, and they want to ensure their members "keep up."

Make time to learn. It doesn't matter if what you're learning has anything to do with your job or not—I'm often dismayed at people who think learning is something that only happens on-the-job— just learn something. Always be learning something. Look at your apprentice audience, and ask what else they might need to learn. Perhaps the people you're sharing work-a-day knowledge with might also want to learn to be leaders or managers one day? Learn how, so that you can help teach them, at least a little. Have they asked something you don't know the answer to? Learn it, perhaps even together, so that you can both teach other something about the process of learning itself.

As Einstein said, "Once you stop learning, you start dying."

Masters Improve

While Mastery is much about bringing up the next generation in a particular trade or topic, it's also about *furthering* the trade or topic itself.

 ...and this smithy was known for the unique, hoof-saving designs that Timothy's Master had taught him.

This is a lot less difficult than it might initially sound. I'm not talking about changing the way a particular trade works. I'm not suggesting you need to invent some new element to your trade, or a new tool, or anything else. *Improving* something, in the end, is really nothing more than a different kind of sharing-of-information.

Look at it this way: in whatever topic you're thinking of, whether it be a hobby, something you do at work, or some other part of your life, you've probably learned how to do it through some combination of experience, trial-and-error, and learning from other people, right?

I'm no plumber. I would never consider myself a Master Plumber. But I did take it upon myself, once upon a time, to install a water softener in my house. Now, my house had been plumbed for a water softener, which is to say I had a loop of copper piping coming out of the wall in the garage, looping back, and going back into the wall. The builder's theory was that some plumber could come in, cut the loop so it was just two pipes coming out of the wall, and solder threaded connectors onto the pipe. They could then roll up a water softener and screw its tubes into those pipes, and I'd be good to go. Simple, right? Perfect DIY project, right? Heh.

I actually got the first threaded connector soldered on just fine. That was the end the water goes *into* the wall—the "demand" side, I call it. That's probably not an official plumbing term. Soldering pipe isn't actually that hard: you sand down the pipe a bit, rub some rosin on it, and stick the fitting on. You hold a torch over it to heat it up, and then hold a piece of solder up to the seam. The solder melts and gets "sucked" into the joint, and you're good. So long as you don't see any steam, that is: steam indicates the pipe wasn't dry, and it'll keep the solder from setting, and you'll have a leak. I read this online.

As I said, the "demand" side went fine. But the damn "supply" side, where the water is meant to come out and *into* the water softener, kept dripping, because we'd only shut the water off an hour or so before. No problem, according to the Intertubez! You go and get a pack of this corn starch-based stuff that plumbers user, and stuff it into the pipe. It absorbs water while you work, but eventually dissolves so there's no blockage. Except I could get it stuffed enough to hold the water back. Hours (and hours) later, I gave up and called a plumber.

"Ah, yeah, there's a special tool for this," he said. Of course there is. He pulls a rubber hose out of his pocket. He sticks the fitting on the pipe, pushes the hose through the fitting into the tube, and *blows* into it, blowing the water back, while he solders the connection. I kid you not.

That is an improvement. And now that I've shared that trick with you, I have actually demonstrated *some* Mastery in the field. Sure, I'm no *expert*, but I know about that improvement and I've disseminated the information, to however small an audience. I didn't *make* the improvement, perhaps, but I'm helping to *improve the field* of do-it-yourself plumbing (if not professional plumbing, since I expect they all know this already).

See what I mean? I didn't necessarily share this with an apprentice, as I don't presently have a Home Improvement Apprentice (oh, the stories I could tell them, though), but I'm helping—just *helping*, mind you—to raise the overall field of DIY Plumbing, just a little bit.

I'm putting the mechanical improvement out there into the world, unashamed of my own failing (and $150 bucks spent), and helping to improve the *field*.

You an do this through writing, perhaps in a blog. Too many people think they only need to blog about what they're paid to do at work. Hogwash. Too many people think there's already enough blogging out there. Also hogwash; I bet *you* had never heard of the rubber hose trick, either, and I bet you've read plenty of blogs. You know the trick now because a source of information you were already looking at—me—shared it with you. You can do the same thing for others. You could make a YouTube video. You could, and I'm not even kidding here, get your community association or whatever together and do a demo evening where you demonstrate that trick for other homeowners who might be interested in a self-installed water softener. This is just more "finding your apprentice audience" and thinking outside the workplace to do so, and then elevating the overall field by teaching them new tricks. You'll also likely encourage *them* to share tricks *they've* learned, which means you've done something additional to help raise the playing field.

When Masters work directly with apprentices, they help uplift those apprentices in the world. When Masters improve an area, and share that improvement generally, they uplift others—and potentially find a new apprentice audience that they'd never considered.

Masters Unite

Even back in medieval times, the Masters of a given trade knew that they were stronger together than apart. They formed the first Guilds to protect their trades. Guilds became a kind of meta-Master, an organization that could maintain the trade's practices and techniques, define standards for bringing up new apprentices, set fair compensation for members' services, and so on. Guilds outlived individual Masters, and became a kind of living memory that allowed our societies to advance and thrive. Over time, labor unions replaced Guilds in some ways, and in some trades, but in many of today's trades we lack the unity and professional oversight that Guilds offered.

I've pointed out that Masters improve, they innovate, and they *share*. When you work in a field that doesn't already have a Guild-like structure, then as a true high-level Master you also have a responsibility to help foster that Guild-like environment. You need to create a place where fellow Masters in your trade can come together and share information, compare notes, and collectively iterate to improve the trade. You need to share experiences, so that you can all, as a group, create progress more quickly than any of you could on your own. You need to create ways of preserving knowledge, techniques, and practices. Ideally, you need to create a way that the world as a whole can recognize your trade's standards, such as creating standardized ways of testing and accepting apprentices into journeyman status.

We see this in many professions in today's world. The State Bar Associations in the United States, for example, perform this exact service for lawyers. Medical Associations do this for various sub-fields of medicine. But we also have many, many trades that don't. If you work in one of those, then as you achieve your own Mastery, know that it should be part of your personal and professional responsibility *to the trade*, if not to your employer, to help create a community for your trade—a modern-day Guild, if you will.

Let me break that down a bit. It's fine if you have a job, and if you're really good at it. But that's just you; it's a selfish accomplishment, really. It's even better if you can share some of that success with others, to help *them* become successful in your trade. That's starting to move beyond your *job* and to think more about your *career* and your *craft*. It's wonderful if you can make improvements in the day-to-day workings of your job. It's *superlative* if you can start to help your trade, as a whole, innovate. You see, that's where you're really starting to rise above a mere single job, and starting to rise into your career, or trade, as a true profession. And when you can then help create, participate in, or maintain a connection between you and other trade practitioners *regardless of your individual employers* then you've achieved true Mastery status. You've elevated your paycheck into something larger than yourself. Something that goes beyond "going to work every day" and into something that will *provide* you with your next job, when the time comes and the need arises. Something that will provide *new people* with a job, because you're helping to collect, preserve, and pass on the information and experiences they need to succeed.

It's when you can say, "you know, this thing that I do for money—this is worthwhile. This is a thing that is important. It has techniques, practices, and a life of its own. I will not only help improve its status, but I will work to bring new people into it, and I will work to connect us all." That's when you've truly reached Mastery.

And it doesn't need to be huge. You don't need to be the one to bring together an entire field of practitioners across the globe. Maybe you're into building plastic models of spaceships, and you and a group of like-minded model buildings get together a couple of times a month to exchange tips and tricks. That's a kind of Mastery, right there. Masters don't need to change the world—there are few pieces of work more humble than a horseshoe—but they're the ones who change *lives*, and who take it upon themselves to create an attitude that others can carry on into the future. Because while horseshoes may be humble, they're still something we need, even today.

Masters Unite

Even back in medieval times, the Masters of a given trade knew that they were stronger together than apart. They formed the first Guilds to protect their trades. Guilds became a kind of meta-Master, an organization that could maintain the trade's practices and techniques, define standards for bringing up new apprentices, set fair compensation for members' services, and so on. Guilds outlived individual Masters, and became a kind of living memory that allowed our societies to advance and thrive. Over time, labor unions replaced Guilds in some ways, and in some trades, but in many of today's trades we lack the unity and professional oversight that Guilds offered.

I've pointed out that Masters improve, they innovate, and they *share.* When you work in a field that doesn't already have a Guild-like structure, then as a true high-level Master you also have a responsibility to help foster that Guild-like environment. You need to create a place where fellow Masters in your trade can come together and share information, compare notes, and collectively iterate to improve the trade. You need to share experiences, so that you can all, as a group, create progress more quickly than any of you could on your own. You need to create ways of preserving knowledge, techniques, and practices. Ideally, you need to create a way that the world as a whole can recognize your trade's standards, such as creating standardized ways of testing and accepting apprentices into journeyman status.

We see this in many professions in today's world. The State Bar Associations in the United States, for example, perform this exact service for lawyers. Medical Associations do this for various sub-fields of medicine. But we also have many, many trades that don't. If you work in one of those, then as you achieve your own Mastery, know that it should be part of your personal and professional responsibility *to the trade*, if not to your employer, to help create a community for your trade—a modern-day Guild, if you will.

Let me break that down a bit. It's fine if you have a job, and if you're really good at it. But that's just you; it's a selfish accomplishment, really. It's even better if you can share some of that success with others, to help *them* become successful in your trade. That's starting to move beyond your *job* and to think more about your *career* and your *craft.* It's wonderful if you can make improvements in the day-to-day workings of your job. It's *superlative* if you can start to help your trade, as a whole, innovate. You see, that's where you're really starting to rise above a mere single job, and starting to rise into your career, or trade, as a true profession. And when you can then help create, participate in, or maintain a connection between you and other trade practitioners *regardless of your individual employers* then you've achieved true Mastery status. You've elevated your paycheck into something larger than yourself. Something that goes beyond "going to work every day" and into something that will *provide* you with your next job, when the time comes and the need arises. Something that will provide *new people* with a job, because you're helping to collect, preserve, and pass on the information and experiences they need to succeed.

It's when you can say, "you know, this thing that I do for money—this is worthwhile. This is a thing that is important. It has techniques, practices, and a life of its own. I will not only help improve its status, but I will work to bring new people into it, and I will work to connect us all." That's when you've truly reached Mastery.

And it doesn't need to be huge. You don't need to be the one to bring together an entire field of practitioners across the globe. Maybe you're into building plastic models of spaceships, and you and a group of like-minded model buildings get together a couple of times a month to exchange tips and tricks. That's a kind of Mastery, right there. Masters don't need to change the world—there are few pieces of work more humble than a horseshoe—but they're the ones who change *lives*, and who take it upon themselves to create an attitude that others can carry on into the future. Because while horseshoes may be humble, they're still something we need, even today.

Masters Leave

The last thing a Master does is one of the hardest, but it's how you know you've met a true, dedicated, die-hard Master.

They leave.

If you're a parent, then you know that almost nothing can be harder than sending your child off into the world, whether it's their first overnight away-from-home school trip, their first out-of-town job, or just their first apartment elsewhere in the same city. There's almost nothing more difficult for a parent than taking this life-form that you created, nurtured, protected, disciplined, fed, bathed, clothed, argued with, and loved, and letting them go off into the world to make their own mistakes. You'll always have a strong instinct to check in on them, give them advice, and try to prevent them from doing something stupid with their lives. But, at the end of the day, your true measure as a parent is whether you can let them go and have them survive on their own. Sure, maybe they won't do things the same way you'd like, but so long as they're surviving and thriving, you did your job.

That's Mastery.

No matter what you create, how much you improve your field, how many apprentices you teach, what innovations you've made, or what you've done to create community within your trade, it's all worthless unless you've built it in a way that you can personally step away from and have others take over.

This is what I've dealt with in recent years, and as I write this chapter I'm fresh in the middle of it. I started teaching about Windows PowerShell, a Microsoft software product used to automate the administration of Microsoft Windows servers and networks, back when the product was introduced in 2006. I feel I've done a good job of bringing people into the field—my books are amongst the best-selling and most-recommended ways for someone to get started with the product. I've improved the field by documenting practices and patterns that work best. I've innovated by helping to improve the product in small ways, and by helping people understand its intricacies. I've literally helped create community around it, in the form of the PowerShell.org website and the in-person PowerShell + DevOps Global Summit event held every year. I've tried to help create an environment where people can use those resources to educate each other, continue to evolve our professional practices as a trade, and to share those practices. Many (truly, a lot) of them have far surpassed me in their expertise with the product, and a good number are now stepping up their own Mastery by sharing what they've learned and developed. And now it's time for me to step away for all of that. If, at this point, it can't keep running without me and the other people who created it, then it wasn't worth doing in the first place and it deserves to fall apart. I hope it won't, and there is certainly a new core group of people who seem ready to step up and keep it going, this little Guild of ours. But even if they don't, just like a parent who's seeing their kid off for the first time, I can't step in. I'll help if they ask for it, of course—what parent wouldn't?—but I need to make sure they have room to make mistakes, enjoy successes, and evolve things into their own vision.

It's hard. It's so hard that it's created arguments amongst those of us who started the things about when the "right time" to step away was. But I'll know that my apprentice audience, the journeymen they've grown to be, and all the work I've done is truly worth it once I'm no longer needed. That, for me, is the pinnacle of Mastery: when you can step back into the shadows and see everything continue to function, evolve, grow, and improve without you.

 ... His Master snorted. "I never could make a proper shield," he said, and walked out.

Interlude: The Grind

Defining your success, your self... all of that can be a little intimidating. And it can be hard to keep up with. That's why I created The Grind for myself. It was a way of keeping myself honest, keeping myself on-track, and keeping myself engaged. You'll want to get the workbook (The Grind workbook is available on Amazon, and members of the BeTheMaster.com mailing list get a print-it-yourself PDF version for free) and follow along.

Using The Grind

To do this, you're going to need the "Be the Master: The Grind" workbook, which is a companion offering to this book. It's a roughly 200-page, spiral-bound book that's designed for a year's worth of monthly and weekly plans and reviews. This chapter is designed to walk you through the process. The workbook is a separate purchase, and should be available on Amazon.com and Lulu.com—visit BeTheMaster.com to find purchasing links.

Believe it or not, The Grind is actually something I've done myself for almost a decade. I was a bit informal about it, to be honest, and I've codified it and generalized it a bit for this book. In fact, writing this has really been an opportunity to think hard about the way I work and organize myself, in a hope that it'll prove useful to others. But your takeaway here is that, while it's important to actually *do* The Grind, you're not a failure just because you took a week off here and there or because you "half-assed" it every so often. I do, too.

My inspiration for The Grind came from the Steven Covey methodology and all the FranklinCovey DayRunner-type things. My problem is that I was nowhere near disciplined enough to do those things every day, and barely even every week. And they were more about time management, in my mind. I needed something to keep me more focused on my long-term aspirations, and so I kind of fiddled around until I came up with something that works. I call it The Grind because it's not necessarily something you do for fun; you do it because you need to.

Here's a thing, though: including previous editions and print and ebook sales, *Be the Master* has sold thousands of copies. But I know very, very, very few people are doing "The Grind." That's fine; I know, anecdotally, that plenty of people are taking what works for them from this book and using it, and that's really all I can ask for. But I know a lot of people got this book and then... maybe didn't even read this far. Or did, but deferred doing anything about it in their own lives.

Please don't do that.

Here's a quote from the original blog post that started this whole book:

> ...you should not be learning anything about your trade from other people unless you plan to teach it to other people. The point is preserving knowledge and continuing the craft. People don't help you just so you can get a better job and so you can live a better life. If there's one thing that infuriates me about online Q&A forums, it's the number of people who sail in, ask people to spend valuable time solving their problem, and then vanish into obscurity. Without giving back.
>
> Teaching does not always feel rewarding. It doesn't need to be. It is a repayment of something that was done for you. It is not a good thing that you do; it is an obligation that you have. If you are not preserving and expanding your trade, then you are a leech, and you do not deserve to prosper in it.

You see, I haven't taken the time to write all this stuff down to help readers improve their own lives. I'm not even sure how much of this *would* help someone improve their own lives. This book is all about getting you to the point *where you can help others' lives.* That's the priority. You are, if I'm being blunt, a means to an end. A positive end, to be sure, with a rewarding journey along the way. But **if you don't DO this stuff, then none of the benefit happens.** The reason I selfishly want *everyone* to be doing The Grind is because I know it'll get us all helping one another.

So please. *Please.* Follow along.

Step 1: Define The Grind

The first part of the workbook has you complete five sections. Most of these are designed to be perpetual, in the sense that you'll be constantly revising them, adding to them, and so on. I suggest using pencil, not pen. And if you're not interesting in buying the workbook, it's totally fine. You can do this on plain paper, in your favorite note-taking app, or wherever else.

Define Yourself

The **Who am I?** section comes directly from the "Define Yourself" chapter in Part 3 of this book. Make statements about *who you are* or *who you want to be*. Again, these need to be externally observable, objectively measurable statements. These go beyond your career and job and should touch on every element of your life.

- I provide comfortable shelter and other necessities for my family.
- I provide at least two weeks of away-from-home vacation every year for my family.
- I volunteer several hours a week for the local homeless shelter.
- I help lead the Women in Leadership group for my company.

Make as many of these statements as you want to. Some can be aspirational—things you don't do now that you want to add to your life. But review the final list carefully because, as described in the "Define Yourself" chapter, it's easy to make a list that no mortal could possibly live up to. It's fine to make statements, master those, and then add more later, so don't feel you need to define your entire adult life here.

And remember, this isn't necessarily about *goals*. I view a goal as something you do, and which is then done. Defining yourself isn't something you do and then stop doing; it's *who you are*. It describes your everyday life, your personal values, and your core concerns.

Know Yourself

Next, complete **What are my strengths?** This section is where you list the things that you do *really* well, almost without effort. Ask other people around you for ideas, here, and don't feel like you're bragging or being arrogant. Just be honest. Again, try to focus on strengths that *anyone* could confirm or deny, if they knew you, lived with you, or worked with you.

- I relate well to people.
- I am extremely aware of deadlines.
- I task-switch easily and well.
- People enjoy talking to me.
- I write incredibly quickly.

It's important to list these things because your plan is going to work best if you line it up around these strengths. Think of it this way: Suppose you tell an engineer that you need to get citizens easily back and forth across a river. That's a Success statement: "Citizens can easily move from one side of the river to the other." It's a measurable outcome, and you can put a deadline on it. The engineer now has to figure out what strengths they have to work with. In a mineral-poor area with swampy riverbanks, a big metal suspension bridge might not be the best plan. Instead, the local strengths might play more to wooden ferries. By understanding those strengths, the engineer can make a plan that achieves the goal.

You're the same way. Your success goals are going to be more easily achieved if you attack them *using your strengths*, and so you need to know what those strengths are.

Think about your strengths in a series of categories, from Part 3:

- What are your learning strengths?
- What are your work/job strengths?
- What are your personality strengths?

This is also not a bad time to think about *aspirational strengths.* Perhaps you'd like to be a good teacher but you don't think you are, right now. Don't write that down in the strengths section, though. Instead, decide how that aspiration fits into your overall success. Is being a good teacher part of that success or something you need in order to achieve the rest of your success? If so, turn that aspiration into a proper Success statement: "By the end of 2021, I will have taught two in-person courses in my field and have received 80% or better student ratings." Once you achieve that, maybe "I am a good teacher" can be added to your list of strengths.

It's also a good idea to document your weaknesses, especially those that you feel might stand in the way of you living the life you want. Write them down. This doesn't mean you have to fix them all; sometimes you might say, "you know what, I'm fine with that. I'll adjust my definition of self to accommodate that, because I don't want to change." That's fine: it's *you* making a decision about yourself and your life. The important thing is to *make it a decision,* not just leave it unacknowledged.

Define Success

Go back to the "Achieve Your Success" Part of this book and read about defining your success. What *is* yours? This needs to be your "North Star," the thing you're always aligning to. *Write it down.*

Human brains learn by creating synaptic networks between the neurons in our brain. Those neurons live in different parts of the brain, many of which are associated with our six senses. The more senses you involve in something, the more neurons that "light up," and the stronger and more forceful the resulting feelings and memories are.

By *writing things down* in The Grind workbook, you're engaging more senses than if you just typed into a fill-in PDF. Writing, for most of us, is a more physically thoughtful process, since we don't rely on the muscle memory that enables touch-typing.

This is worth the extra time. Indeed, the extra time is part of what makes this exercise so valuable.

There is a key difference between your Success Definition and your Self Definition. Your success is something you will, someday, achieve and leave behind. Even if you're constantly evolving your vision of success, it remains something to be *achieved*; it is a *goal*. Your self-definition, in contrast, is something *you strive to be all the time*. You don't do it and then quit; you *always* do it. The two are related, though: You can't self-define as someone who makes it to the kids' soccer games every week but define your success as a jet-setting, globetrotting consultant who is never home. They're not compatible.

De-Conflict

So, you also need to reconcile this list against your Success statements. If you've decided that your success will include "By the end of 2020, I will have taught at least one class in each of twelve countries around the world," and you've made a defining statement like, "I will always be home for my family," then one of your strengths had better be, "I can clone myself." Don't create unrealistic expectations for yourself. You'll end up failing, which will demoralize you and jeopardize *everything*. If anything, it's better to start a little conservatively, and then build up more and more as you gain your stride and learn more about what you can actually pull off.

Identify Milestones

Once you've hopped in a car and punched a destination into the GPS, what does the GPS do? It creates a route for you. So that's what you need to do next, and a good way to do that is to define some milestones. I wrote about this in the "Define Success" Part of this book, so it's worth going back and rereading that.

However, to briefly summarize: your success is your "end state." It's where you want to be at the end of your career, life, or whatever. Milestones are your GPS route for getting there. They're the big intermediate goals you work toward, knowing that if you hit them all, you'll also hit your success. Put dates on your milestones, to give yourself something to work toward.

I use the Milestones section of The Grind to document these things, and I use *pen*, because I often find myself wanting to adjust them. Don't. Push yourself toward those goals. Next year, when you start a new The Grind workbook, you can make any adjustments based on the prior year.

Define Your Teaching Catalog

In **What can I teach?**, start making a list of things you can teach. This may start simple:

- How to change a tire
- How to balance a bank account
- How to negotiate for a new car
- How to read real estate listings

Basic life skills count here! Over time, you'll fill in more and more things. Think about things at your job, too, even if they're specific to your current employer:

- Manage invoicing in proprietary system
- Core SQL Server database administration
- Rebuild an automatic transmission

And only include things you actually *enjoy*. Like, if you'd rather eat a spider than change a tire, don't write "Change a tire" on your list. And this list doesn't just need to be high-end, world-changing things. Remember, you're not here to compare yourself to your gurus, Masters, or people who taught *you*. You're not comparing yourself to *anyone*. Remember Timothy the blacksmith? His Master couldn't teach him to make a shield but that didn't mean there were other things his Master couldn't teach. Horseshoes might not have been sexy, but they were *useful*. Timothy's Master may not have set him up to be a wartime blacksmith, but he taught him plenty of useful things, and Timothy could always work with *another* Master, at another time, if he wanted to learn something else. Point being, focus on what you *can* teach, not on what you *can't.*

Really focusing on *what can I teach* is an exercise in thinking about *what do I know how to do well*. That, in turn, can help you tremendously with the next step, which is thinking about *who I can teach*. You may find, for example, that the things you can teach, and that you might enjoy teaching, aren't things your immediate colleagues at work need you to teach. That's fine—that's a cue to start looking outside that audience to other audiences.

Define Your Apprentice Audience

Finally, start thinking about **who are my apprentices?** These are ideas for people who might be in, or adjacent to, your life who could benefit from the things *you can already teach*.

I'm going to make a big deal of that.

People who need what you can already teach. You see, in The Grind, you're not allowed to put off teaching until you finally feel expert enough in something you feel is "worthy" enough, whatever that means. You need to start teaching **now**. It's going to be part of your Weekly Reviews, in fact. That means you need to start examining what you *can* teach and then *find an audience for it.* Is changing tires your only strong suit right now? That's fine—find a local club for kids and teach them how to change tires. It's never too early to learn certain life skills—you just need to find the audience that's in need of learning them.

Your apprentice-candidate list will change over time as you grow capable of teaching more things. After you really nail down your house-building skills, you can make that trip to a disadvantaged country and teach people there how to build houses. That's a huge, objectively "worthy" thing to do - but just because you can't do it *yet* doesn't mean you can put off serving as Master to some other group of apprentices.

Be wary of *manufacturing* an audience of apprentices, though. "I like to cook, and I know a lot of people in my apartment building don't cook, so I'm going to hold cooking classes for them!" This can work out great sometimes, but it can also wind up being a huge disappointment when two people show up for one class, and then nobody shows up for the next one. You need to *find* your audience, not assume they'll show up. Canvass the building and see who does, in fact, want to learn to cook. Maybe you *do* have an audience there, but *validate* that hypothesis first. And if you don't, you can still teach cooking! You just need to go find the audience that's waiting for you to teach them. That audience may be outside your usual social circles, so start expanding those circles a bit. Find your audience.

Review Your Definitions

The five sections in the front of The Grind all kind of feed on and depend on each other. When you're done, spend some more time reading everything back to yourself. Make sure it makes sense and seems to fit into a whole.

Are there things you'd like to teach but can't yet? Then those should become goals—what success do you need to achieve, in those topics, until you can teach them? Are there things you can teach but have no audience to teach them to? Then you need to do more work on your apprentice-prospect list, because you should be teaching *all that you practically can* to *someone, somewhere.*

 As part of your monthly review and planning session, come back and re-read the first five sections of The Grind. Update where necessary, revise where needed, but most importantly just *re-read* so that these things are in your head, all the time.

Step 2: Monthly Plans

At the end of each month, you're going to review your prior month's performance (obviously, you won't do this in your very first month), and create your plan for the coming month.

Life Rules

There's a handy checklist with the Life Rules from Part 4 of this book. *Did you truly live by these rules?* If so, check 'em off. If not, have a good long think about *why*. And maybe you've decided one or more of these rules aren't for you. That's completely fine—just cross it out completely. Although, before you do that, please do think really hard about it. Don't cross it out just because it's hard. Make sure you understand the rule, and that it truly has no benefit or applicability to your life.

Life Rules you're not meeting are possible items for inclusion on the Needs Improvement list.

Needs Improvement

This is where you document everything that you feel you need to improve, in yourself, in order to better reach your Success statements. Perhaps it's just not living the Life Rules. Perhaps it's that you're making excuses for yourself. Perhaps you're not living the definition of yourself that you wrote down in the first part of The Grind. Maybe you're not leveraging your strengths as well as you could. Whatever it is, list those things here.

These need to get worked into your plan for the next month. Ideally, try to think of situations where a particular weakness will exhibit itself, and then brainstorm ways to improve your performance in those situations. Create a plan to try to *put yourself,* deliberately, into those situations so that you can actively work on your weakness.

It's perfectly fine to list a bunch of Needs Improvement items, but only plan to work on one or two at a time. In fact, I recommend that exact approach. Keep rolling the others over from month to month until you're happier with your performance in that area.

Let's also be clear that Needs Improvement items are things that *drastically* need improvement, especially if they relate to the Life Rules. Just because you were late to the kids' soccer practice a couple of times last quarter doesn't mean you write down "I need to improve my soccer practice attendance." We're looking for the big-ticket items here. And by that same token, plan to remove items once you've *significantly* addressed them. You're not looking for perfection! You're looking for a consistent pattern of improvement until a Needs Improvement item is no longer a major anchor in your life. You'll *always* keep trying to be a little better (or always should be, at least), but when you hit the 90% zone, or thereabouts, start spending time on another major effort.

My Current Plan

This is your months-long plan to achieve your success. It needs to take into account any changes that you've made notes about in your Weekly Reviews, any Needs Improvement items you'd like to work on, and so on. Most importantly, it should contain *specific actions and tasks* that you want to try to complete in order to take the next step toward one or more of your success goals.

Writing down the plan is a physical way of creating stronger neural connections in your brain. *Reading* your plan every night before bed is a way of cueing your brain to be thinking, "How can I make this happen tomorrow?" *Actively work on your plan.* Every time you make a decision to do something, or not to do something, ask, "How is this helping, hurting, delaying, or achieving my plan?"

The plan isn't meant to be a way of making you 100% focused only on your own success. It isn't meant to prevent you from taking vacations. It's meant to make you a *driver in your own life* by making you *make decisions* rather than simply letting things happen to you. Going on vacation and not focusing on the plan is *fine* provided *you decide to do so.* You've made a judgment call. A compromise. That's an adult and laudable thing to do. But without the plan, written down and in front of you, you're still going to be making compromises and decisions - you just won't *know* you're making them. You'll be a passenger in your own life, not the driver.

Step 3: Weekly Plans

This is really where the tires hit the asphalt in your life. The Grind contains 52 Weekly Plan sheets. The idea is to take the Monthly Plan and break it down into manageable chunks. A week is a period of time all of us can grasp. It's not so far into the future that we lose track of it, and it's not an OCD level of granularity that a daily plan would involve. A Weekly Plan provides some wiggle room to deal with the unexpected, allowing us to still accomplish things without daily disappointment.

Start by listing things you want to achieve this week. As always, be actionable and list things that could be objectively observed and measured by anyone. And **you've only got a week**. This is really an exercise in coming to understand what you can actually accomplish in that short timeframe, and developing realistic expectations of yourself.

Everything you want to achieve should line up to either:

- A Success statement
- A Needs Improvement statement

This is *not* meant to be a to-do list for the week. Don't write, "make the mortgage payment." Yes, that might support your self-definition of "provides comfortable housing for my family," but it's not big-picture. If you've been failing to provide that comfortable housing, then I'd hope you'd note that as a Needs Improvement item, and *then* it becomes a weekly achievement goal.

Let's also be clear that, in a single week, you are not going to meet all of your success goals nor are you going to finish your entire life plan. What you're doing with the Weekly Plan is making a conscious decision on *which bits to tackle right now*. This mental exercise lets you do some sequencing and prioritization. For example, if one of your Success statements is to "deliver a presentation to five other people," great. You might, at this point in your life, not feel comfortable giving that presentation. So one of your weekly achievements might be to simply watch a couple of good videos on presentation skills, that's not a hard thing to accomplish. You can probably fit it into your weekly life, and it *furthers the plan.* It links directly back to one of your Success statements, and it might help address a Needs Improvement item like "Be better at public speaking." It addresses one of the Life Rules, too, about communicating. So it's a *great,* eminently achievable item for your Weekly Plan.

Step 4: Weekly Reviews

Last up are the 52 Weekly Review sheets in The Grind. The Week 10 Review is, for example, based on your Week 10 Plan. So you'd do the Week 10 plan at the *start* of Week 10, perhaps on Sunday or Monday, and the Week 10 Review at the *end* of Week 10, on Friday or Saturday.

 I usually do the prior-week review and the next-week plan at the same time. It helps me carry over items from the previous week, and it's a good time to spot any patterns that I want to take an active hand in changing.

Start your review by going back to the Weekly Plan and highlighting (yes, get a highlighter) any achievements you actually achieved. For the rest, decide what you're going to do about them. Will they roll into the next week? Will you modify them? Will you drop them? Make a short note next to each on what you did, such as "ROLLED" or "DROPPED."

Next, on the Weekly Review sheet, write down any Needs Improvement items that you worked on. How'd it go? Have you improved any of these sufficiently to consider removing them from the Needs Improvement list next month?

Make some notes about how your Weekly Plan went, and how you might want to adjust your Monthly Plan for next month. You're not doing so yet, but this is a good spot to indicate where maybe something was harder or would take longer than you expected. This is where you gather evidence about how well the plan is working and what might need to evolve next month.

List parts of your self-definition that you don't think you lived this week. These are candidates for the Needs Improvement list next week. This can include any Life Rules you feel you didn't live up to.

What did you teach this week, and to whom did you teach it? Teaching should be an almost daily task for someone becoming a Master, and this is a good spot to review your performance. Did you teach something new to someone in a new audience? Make sure you're updating the front sections of The Grind with those new topics and audience ideas.

Finally, what excuses did you make, and what did they stop you from doing? Sometimes, excuses are fine. If you had a really bad week and just decided to drop a few weekly achievement items, that's acceptable. Just *document* that you did so. Here's why: If you start seeing a pattern in yourself, then you need to adjust your plan accordingly. Don't "plan" to write a magazine article per month when you've dropped it four months in a row. That's just lying to yourself. A *pattern* of repeated excuses means you either need to adjust your plan (because your plan was wrong), or you've perhaps aimed too high (which again means adjusting your plan). Sometimes a pattern can indicate that you're simply cheating yourself—and you need to call yourself on it and decide what to do about it.

And when (not if) you do adjust your plan, be sure you're adjusting *all the way back* to the sections in the front of The Grind. If you're no longer going to be taking actions that were intended to lead to a success goal, then maybe you should think about whether that success goal is still appropriate. If your plans no longer have you actively working toward something, then that something might not be a personal goal anymore. Of course, maybe it *is* still a goal—but a goal for a future time, not right now. That means adjusting your success list to update your timelines and deadlines. That's fine.

I also use my Weekly Review time, every three or four weeks, to go back and re-read my Success statements from the front of The Grind. It's a way to make sure that my success goals are firmly in mind, and that I'm not letting my Monthly and Weekly Plans go off on some kind of tangent. It helps me keep everything lined up to the end goal, and helps keep that end goal firmly in my mind.

Create a Powerful Driving Habit

Habits are hard to form. They take a long time, which is why they take a long time to break, too. And habits form *only* through repetition. So whether you're using the actual workbook or not, make The Grind a habit. That's going to take active, conscious effort at first. It's worth it. This will put you in the driver's seat of your life. You'll be making decisions, setting a course, and in control the whole way. You won't be a passive passenger, just waiting for things to happen to you. *This is worth the effort,* I promise.

And there's another thing. One company I've worked for speaks in terms of *leading powerfully* when they bring new leaders into the company, or when they promote someone. I don't love the phrase, but I love the meaning. Basically, it's this: once you've set out a path or plan for yourself, you can proceed with two kinds of thoughts and actions. *Powerful* thoughts and actions help you progress on your plan; *non-powerful* thoughts and actions do not help you progress on your plan.

You can choose to get inside your own head and put a stop to non-powerful thoughts and actions. It's a big part of what the Weekly Reviews are all about, but it's something you can do on a daily basis. *How are you sabotaging yourself?* It's terrible to think, let alone say, that you "can't" do something that you need to do. It's fine to say, "I don't know how right now," because that creates a path where you can learn how. It's sort-of fine to say, "I am choosing not to right now," because that's a choice. But whatever you do, you have to focus on making The Grind a *powerful* activity.

The idea is to set down for some "me time" every week—not much, just a few minutes—and make sure the car of your life is pointed in the direction you want it to go. Don't let things *happen* to your life. *Make* them happen, by deliberate, thoughtful, powerful choices.

Part VI: The Nine Rules of Life

I don't necessarily think that life is an easy thing to succeed at, but I do believe it's straightforward. These are the rules I've adopted, mostly by watching the people I admire *as people* go about their lives.

Be Your Word

I've always had three simple rules that have, I tell myself, contributed greatly to my success in business and in life. These may, in fact, be the Big Three that tell you everything you need to know.

First is … actually, no. Here's the problem: You're going to read these and, more than anything else in this book, think, "Well, duh." But these aren't "of course" rules. They're demonstrably not common sense *because they're not that common*. Following these have enabled me, and past business partners, to rise above the crowd simply because, as simple as these rules are, *almost nobody follows them*.

1: Never Promise What You Can't Deliver

Simple rule. Hard to follow. Here's why: Most people don't want to be the bearer of bad news. If someone asks you to do something, and you say "no," then they're going to want to know why. Now you're going to feel like you're in a confrontation. Most people hate confrontation, so they'll say, "yes," instead, essentially kicking the can down the road. People will say "yes" even *knowing full well* that they can't actually deliver on what they've promised.

So you need to get better at saying "no" *without* making it a confrontation. "No, because I'm already max committed. If I take on something else, I'll need to drop something I've already committed to do." Or, "No because I just really don't want to." Whatever the reason, don't say "yes" unless you will actually, for sure, definitely be able to deliver. Don't say "yes" thinking, *well, I can probably cram this in someplace.* Only say "yes" if you have a definite, workable, practical, realistic plan for making it happen.

2: Always Deliver What You Promised

The companion of the first rule. If you did promise something, no matter what was going through your head at the time, then *you have to deliver it.* Period.

I've had colleagues who've *literally* used the "my dog ate my PowerPoints that were on a USB drive" excuse. Know how much respect they get? That's right. Not delivering on something you've promised is a *lie*, and people do not respect liars. People do not respect excuses. You don't either, right? Someone commits to do something for you, and you want them to do it. So you have to do the same thing.

If you've been dumb and overcommitted, deliver anyway. Don't sleep. Be miserable—I don't care. Deliver on your promises. Maybe your misery will teach you to say "no" now and then, and not commit to things you can't deliver.

There is definitely a life skill involved here that I don't want to gloss over, which is, *know what you can do.* If I asked you to sit down and write a 10-page paper on something, how long would it take you? Do you know? Do you know *for sure?* Because way too many people simply don't pay attention to how long it takes them to accomplish things. This leads them to not understanding what a commitment will actually involve, which leads them to overcommitting, which leads them to telling excuses, which leads them to being a *liar.*

Know yourself.

3: Be Easy to Work With

In business, this was "be easier to work with than the customer just doing it themselves," but it applies more broadly to life. If you commit to doing something, then make it as turnkey as possible. I shouldn't have to bug you. I shouldn't have to nag. I shouldn't have to remind. I shouldn't have to tell you how to do it. I shouldn't get it half-assed from you, get into a fight with you, and make you redo it.

This means paying your bills on time. Nay, ahead of time. Tend to forget? Well, "plan to fail" and schedule automated payments or set reminders. Whatever you commit to, commit to doing it as right as possible, the first time, and having it in *early* so you've got wiggle room if it needs to be redone or fixed.

Easy, right? Sure. Except, ask yourself how many times you've personally violated any one of these three rules. Be honest with yourself. *Brutally* honest—if you can't admit your faults to yourself, then you can't ever succeed at anything. Not truly. So take a hard look in the mirror and ask if these three rules are ones you truly live by in every aspect of your life.

Be your word. Nearly all of my success has come from these three simple rules.

Be Detailed and Precise

Human brains have this good-and-bad little feature called *filtering*. This is a deeply embedded feature, designed first and foremost to help ensure our primitive ancestors' survival in the wild. When you've the potential to become someone else's lunch, your brain has to quickly decide what, in your immediate environment, is important, and what isn't. It needs to discard the unimportant things ("ooo, pretty tree") and focus sharply on the important things ("something is stalking me"). This can't be done as part of your conscious thought because that would take too long; it has to happen automatically, constantly, and almost instantly.

Recognize that: You can't shut off the filtering system any more than you cut shut off your own heartbeat.

But, like your heartbeat, you can exercise *control* over the feature. For example, calm, deep breathing can help you slow and steady your heart rate. Physical training can help you moderate your heart rate and help your heart respond more appropriately to a given situation. Same with the filter: With some *active training*, you can help your brain do a better job of deciding what's important, and prevent the filter from trapping information that it should really be letting through.

Here's why: We're not primitive hunter-gatherers focused on basic survival anymore. When I meet someone who asks how I like my "iWatch," I immediately make a whole bunch of assumptions about them. One, I don't like them. Two, I don't trust them. It's an *Apple Watch*, not an "iWatch." Now, you may very reasonably be thinking, "Don's kind of being a jerk, here—I mean, who cares?" You'd perhaps be right. But *I* care, and I'll tell you why: To me, this is indeed a very minor detail, so why not get it right? I mean, exactly how much extra brainpower would be required to remember the correct product name? None at all. And given that no extra brainpower or smarts is required, all I can imagine is that *this person isn't very good at paying attention to details.* Then, I think, *I wonder what else they consistently get wrong.* They don't have control over their filter, so what else about themselves can't they control?

First (and second, and third) impressions are important, and there are myriad ways that you can "put off" other people. Many people have an instinctive distrust of someone who seems sloppy, for example, and that can extend to your attention to detail. If you can't get the little things right, you're likely to not get the big things right, either.

Details come up all the time in our daily lives. Start paying attention to the stores that you shop, and how they merchandise (arrange) the products on their shelves. Are things neatly arranged, sensibly organized, and attractively displayed? If so, there's probably a lot more going on right behind the scenes. I'd never shop in a badly merchandised grocery store because if you can't keep the front pretty—the place, you, as a store manager, *know* customers can see—then there are probably cockroaches running things in the back. Sure, a few misplaced containers of Tide doesn't necessarily *mean* that you have a major alien infestation in the butcher department ... but I'm not the kind to take chances.

Do you trust yourself to do your own income tax returns? I do because I know I pay a lot of attention to the details. I know I can be careful about reading instructions, not gloss over things, and stop to investigate if I run across something I'm unsure of. If I hadn't trained my brain filter, though, I'm not sure I would trust myself. Taxes are one of those things you can't miss a bit on, and if I wasn't accustomed to really focusing on small details, I'd be afraid I'd miss something. I'd have someone else do my taxes, like many people do, even though I've no evidence that they're any more detailed than myself. And, in doing so, I'd give up control over a major aspect of my own life, trusting it to a stranger. (As a sidebar, it amazes me that people will entrust tens of thousands of dollars of financial obligation to a stranger in a shopping strip tax shop but get all bent out of shape about who babysits their *pet*. Odd priorities.)

As you move through life, know that perhaps the most important bit of self-ownership you can have is over that brain filter of yours. Train it to *obey* you. Teach it *not* to filter out small details. Let those details flow over you and *actively* decide what you need to pay attention to. Don't let some 5,000 B.C.E. caveman decide what you're going to pay attention to.

How?

Slow down. Our brain filters are designed to quickly assess fast-moving situations. They're literally designed to keep us alive during the hunt. Our modern world being so much more full of potential distractions, it's easy for our brain filters to just shut it all out. Consider airports, one of the most frenetic and distraction-rich environments you can possibly imagine. The damn overhead public address systems are always spouting something, you're rushing to your plane, people are everywhere and you're trying to dodge them, and your brain filters go into high gear. You start ignoring literally anything that isn't an immediate threat or obstacle. Admit it: You could be dashing to your flight and they could announce the recipe to curing cancer over the P.A. system, and you'd miss it.

Slow down.

Once your body is no longer in a mad rush, your brain filters will relax. Once your body doesn't feel like it's in a fight-or-flight situation, the survival filters aren't as necessary, and so they'll chill out. Your tunnel vision will expand to include more of the world, and your brain will become more observant. This means you're going to have to *actively allow yourself to slow down*. Leave 10 minutes earlier for that appointment. Get to the airport half an hour earlier, and allow for a longer connection. *Don't rush*. Over time, your brain filters will become less hair-triggered, and you'll be able to speed things up a bit more without going into Full Filter

Lockdown again. Your brain's hindparts will realize that you're not in the hunt and that moving quickly isn't a survival threat, and so your brain won't bother engaging the filters as strongly. You'll pick up more detail—and in our modern world, *details* are the key to survival and success.

You see, this is very much a case where the things our brains did to keep us alive in the caves *works exactly against us* in our modern, cave-less world. Details *are* survival, now, as we have ever-more detailed and critical interactions with each other, with technology, and with our environments. *Care* about the details. A lack of attention to detail is what makes phishing email scams work. It's what makes nearly every scam possible, in fact. It's what causes car accidents. It's what makes you miss your train. Nearly everything that can go wrong in your life can be traced back to a lack of attention to detail. So train yourself to "read the fine print of life" all the time. If you find yourself skimming, *stop*, go back, and do it again more slowly. *Focus* on absorbing details, instead of letting your brain just do whatever it wants.

Be detail-oriented.

Cut Your Losses When the Time Is Right

I have a friend who, not too long ago, had to go through bankruptcy proceedings. It was a complicated situation and not entirely of his own making; family, sometimes, can drag you down unnecessarily. His bankruptcy gave him the space to make good on his financial obligations and taught him some valuable life lessons. What was strange to me, though, is that he never brought his house into it. He'd bought high – very high – in the boom of 2007, and was deeply underwater by 2009. But he never even considered trying to restructure the debt on his house, as so many people were doing at the time, even though he was struggling to make ends meet.

We spoke about it on several occasions, and it basically came down to this: His attorney advised him that, in order to get the bank to consider a restructure and write-down, he'd have to stop paying his mortgage. So long as he was paying, the bank had no reason to even consider the situation. Simply stopping payments, for him, was unacceptable. It meant, to him, that he'd failed. He felt that way on a very deep emotional level that's hard to overcome with mere facts, even though he intellectually understood the situation very well. It was another two years before he was finally desperate enough to take the plunge, and the bank did indeed drop his interest rate and write off a significant portion of his principal.

Before he'd taken that plunge, he and I had spoken—again, at some length – about his broader emotions around the house. He didn't want to live there, he'd confided. He was done with the house. It represented a bad time for him, and he just wanted *out*. Being upside-down as he was, selling simply wasn't an option. I asked at the time if he'd considered just walking away, as so many others have done, and letting the bank foreclose. Now, whether *you*, dear reader, think that's an honorable act or not isn't my point. My point is that my friend simply *refused* to even consider the option because it, once again, represented a *massive failure* to him.

So what's this mean to you? Well, on a smaller scale, we're all faced with similar situations every day. We get into a situation of some kind that just isn't ideal and isn't "furthering the mission," and we have two options. One is to doggedly keep at it, and the other is to cut your losses and do something else. *Neither* of these is *always* the right answer to every situation. Instead, it's always a fine, vague line that we have to find in ourselves. Simply giving up on everything at the slightest hint of resistance isn't useful; nothing beneficial comes to us without some work and effort. However, continuing to bang your head against a brick wall for no reason also isn't useful, unless you're just a fan of bloody foreheads. I find that one of the most useful life skills you can have is *knowing when to quit.*

Our brains don't like us to quit. Fear avoidance can kick in, making us feel like a failure. Nobody likes to feel like a failure, and we often resist that feeling more powerfully than we would pursue a feeling of success. This, in fact, is a big thing that holds most people back in their lives: **Rather than risk the feeling of failure, we will content ourselves with a lack of success.**

I've had failures. I didn't go to college, but I did complete a four-year apprenticeship as an aircraft mechanic. I then walked away from that "career" entirely. I wasted four years of my life, by some reckonings. I *failed.* But the job wasn't for me; it wasn't lining me up toward anything I wanted to do. It made me miserable in the day-to-day and it felt like, at the ripe old age of 22, I'd entered a dead end that'd last my entire life. Having given up on that "career," I struggled to do more than find a "job of the moment" for a long time. Looking back, I should have quit that damn apprenticeship two years in, when I *knew* I wasn't going to be happy putting airplanes together for the rest of my life. I should have cut my losses and run, spent some time thinking about who I actually wanted to be, and pursued that. But, at that age, I was terrible at finding the line between quitting too early and cutting my losses. I'm a little better at it now, I think, but you never know until years later if you made the right call in any situation. That's just life.

Incidentally, the career I'd *first* wanted, before the aircraft thing, was computer programming. I was told by more than a few guidance counselors that I wasn't good enough at higher math. The aircraft mechanic apprenticeship was more an act of desperation: they were offering a job, I was a senior in high school, and I had few good prospects. If you know me, then you know that I ultimately found my success, and then some, in the exact field I was told I couldn't succeed in.

Never let someone else tell you what you can succeed at.

You've probably heard Facebook's catch phrase, "Move fast and break things." That's part of what "cut your losses" means. It means you tried something, but you're not going to *keep* trying it past the point of viability, right? Look at the *major* investments companies like Google have made, and subsequently walked away from entirely. Google Wave (whatever that was). Google+ (more or less). You try something, and if you can't make it work, you move on.

Yeah, cutting and running is a kind of failure. Be okay with that. It's not *bad* to fail. It's how we learn. It's not bad to fail and *lose*, if you've come to the point where *winning* is just not going to be practical. Businesses do it all the time, and while bankruptcy can be scary, sometimes it's the legitimate thing to do. Cut your losses, reorganize, and try again.

Be Friendly in the Face of Adversity

We all get into situations where someone else can't, or won't, give us what we want. It might be something we need another team at work to do, or it might be returning an article of clothing to a store. We've *all* seen how a lot of people handle those situations, right? They get aggressive. They get demanding. They want to talk to the manager. They want to fly over everyone's heads to the highest authority. And those people often get *the bare minimum needed to shut them up*. Don't be that person.

You also can't do what I do, which is get kind of passively sarcastic. I'm wired for it, unfortunately, and I really have to watch myself. You also can't be pandering, which is basically a kind of advanced sarcasm. You don't need to be weak, either, which is what a lot of people take to be the opposite of aggressive. In fact, consider the entire possible spectrum between weak and aggressive, and then *step outside it completely.*

Instead, be empathetic. Don't go into a situation wanting to be the winner because right there you set up the other person to be a loser, and they're going to fight you on that. Immediately start by *volunteering* to almost be the loser: "Hey, I know this is coming out of the blue for you, and my team got blindsided too, and we haven't gotten our heads around this. Can I explain what's happening, and maybe get some ideas from you on what we can do to move ahead a bit?" You're not asking for the world; you're approaching from a position of regret and consternation, and asking for advice and compassion, not a "win." "Hey, we didn't keep the receipt for this, and we cut the tags off. We were stupid. I know you can't do a full refund, but is there anything you're allowed to do to help us out?" Most people are more willing to engage special super powers if you're not *demanding* that they do so. Not always—but in the instances where you're dealing with someone who can't or won't help you, being aggressive isn't often going to change that.

"Hey, I really apologize for all these passengers getting in your face, Miss. You must be just as stressed as we are. Can I just tell you what I'm looking at, and maybe get some advice from you?" I've had to say something similar more than a few times at an airport, and I nearly always get the gate agent's maximum effort, even when they've blown off a bunch of aggressive types demanding to know why the airline allowed it to thunderstorm.

I know this is just all "treat others as you'd have others treat you" Golden Rule stuff, but it's *not* common. Be *uncommon* in your dealings with others. It *will* get you more, in the end, than the alternative.

Let Blue Sky Mode Happen

Don't be a "no," be a "how can we." Don't kill ideas because the first iteration doesn't seem workable. Be an engineer not a road block. Don't use "issue" as a soft way of saying "problem." A negative vibe only holds you back, nobody else.

Disney—I know, I use a lot of Disney analogies—has a process that they go through when they're dreaming up new attractions for their parks. They call it "Blue Sky," and it basically means "the clear blue sky is the limit." During "Blue Sky Discussions," you're not allowed to say "no" to something or to start laying out how it won't work. You just dream. You say, "What if we ..." and engage in pure speculation and invention. You don't worry about the logistics in this phase. You don't express your own likes or dislikes. You just let the ideas come, and everyone in the discussion riffs on each other to evolve the ideas, express new ones, and just *ideate*.

You don't see this often in the normal world. Sit in a conference room at almost any company and suggest a new product, and you'll almost immediately get push-back. Reasons why it can't work. Possible "issues." Roadblocks. Hurdles.

As an aside, I abhor the way we use "issue" in modern conversation. It's meant to be some "less aggressive" way of saying problem, and I just hate "soft" language. If something is a problem, *say so*.

An *issue* is some point of conversation for which there are multiple perspectives, and where no one perspective is objectively right or wrong. Politics have *issues*, for example. Saying, "I have an issue with that" is just modern doublespeak because nobody "wants to be part of the problem."

Well, *don't* be part of the problem. If there is a problem, say so, but don't *be* the problem.

Also, *issue* can be used in reference to magazines, coins, stamps, and offspring. Those are fine.

Don't be that person. Let "Blue Sky Mode" *happen*. Be the person who says, "Oh, it'd be hard, but maybe we could do [whatever] to make that work." Be an engineer of solutions, not an engineer of roadblocks. Your idea for a solution might not be workable, but it's still Blue Sky Mode; let someone else take your nascent idea and pivot it to something that *will* work.

See, what normally happens is someone brings up an idea, and a bunch of other people start to crash it before it's even had a chance to live. Sometimes, this is because they see the idea creating more work for them, and they don't want to do it. Be honest with yourself if that's how you feel. Tossing in "reasons why not" isn't helpful, though, and it just makes *you* the problem. It makes other people *not want to engage* you. It puts you on the outside. Don't worry too much about logistics when an idea is just getting going. Instead, see where the idea goes. And, at the appropriate juncture, if an idea is getting solidified enough, start offering *solutions*. "You know, that would normally take more people than we usually can commit to it—but how about this. What if we [idea]? It might mean doing [alternative detail] instead—would that still hit the intent?"

Bringing a solution (indeed, being the person who *is* a solution) in Blue Sky Mode isn't just useful in those work situations. It doesn't just win you supporters and friends. It's also a way to make your own brain start to think about *doing* instead of *not doing*. Most people's brains are instinctively conservative; when we're confronted with something new, we often push back before we've even really thought about it. That's why most people are so resistant to change. The true *innovators* in our society simply don't say "no." They say, "hmm" and start thinking of a way to say "yes." You have to be on the lookout for that "I don't like new things" push-back that comes from the dark recesses of your brain. Recognize it for what it is, and set it aside. Deal with situations rationally, not emotionally or unconsciously.

Be a person who tries to find the "yes." But above all, don't be the person who tries to squash ideation. Let Blue Sky Mode happen.

Manage Your Time

I both love and hate to-do lists. I love them because, for me, they're a decent way to prioritize what I need to do from moment to moment, and a way to make sure I'm not forgetting things. I use my to-do list in conjunction with my email inbox and my calendar. Any item in my inbox is a to-do, which is why I value "Inbox Zero" so much. And I *schedule time* to work on to-do items. That way, I know when I'm supposed to be doing things, and I can assign meaningful "due dates" (and times) to each to-do item. It's a little OCD. I get that.

But that's not why I hate to-do lists. I hate them because I see *so many* people with those Dayrunner books, making themselves lists, *and then never working the list.* Stuff never gets "done." Frankly, it'd drive me absolutely batshit with anxiety. Which is an important point: I'm *so* OCD about my to-do list representing *actual things I need to do* that I'm very careful not to make the list overly granular, and very careful not to make the list overloaded. I plan a couple of weeks in advance *at most*, usually. Otherwise, the list itself just starts to look huge, and unapproachable, and monstrous, and I stress over it.

I have a dear friend who I walk with quite a bit. We'll sometimes get onto the subjects and jobs and careers, where I obviously have a lot of strongly held opinions. I'll offer suggestions to him, and he'll often say something like, "I'm adding that to my to-do" list.

One time, I asked how long that list was. "Pretty long," he admitted. "Which item are you actively working on right now?" I asked. "None of them, really," he said. "I haven't had time."

"Then why make a list?" I said. Things like "bucket lists" confound me. I understand making a list of far-out things you want to do. I don't understand not beginning to immediately work to make them happen. Why have a list at all?

Again I *get* having a list of long-term things that you're not spending 100% of your time on every single day. I do lists like that. But I *do* work on them. I try to nudge things a little bit every day to aim toward the goals. It would drive me *crazy* not to.

I also manage my time very aggressively. If someone's 5 minutes late for a scheduled meeting and hasn't let me know that the meeting will be delayed, I'm out of there. That's my maximum tolerance for wasted time. I also *track* wasted time. Not the meeting-started-late wasted time, but the time *I waste myself.*

Oh, yeah. I waste time. Everyone does. You *have* to. Human brains *demand* distraction from time to time, just like our bodies do better if we occasionally stand. I swear, I don't know why Apple Watch reminds me to *breath* (have a hypothalamus, I'm good on respiration) and to *stand*, but it can't remind me to go fool around on Facebook for a few minutes. Actually, I'll tell you why: most people start in on Facebook and never stop. Or maybe not Facebook, but something like it. You know what I mean. Maybe your poison is YouTube or Twitter or Chive or whatever, but you've got your pet distraction, and you know you spend too much time on it.

Track that time. I use a "cumulative timer." When I'm about to start wasting time, I start it. I let myself go for five or ten minutes, and then stop it. At the end of the week (or day, whatever), I make a note in my workbook about how much time I wasted that week. This isn't, "oh, that meeting was a waste of time," this is *time I have chosen to waste.* Over a few weeks, I start to find my baseline for wasted time, and so long as I'm tracking around that, I know I'm doing okay. Too little wasted time and I analyze my week to see if I'm feeling stressed, or if I felt less productive, or whatever. Too much, and I focus more on *not wasting as much time* next week. *Wasted time* has a budget for me, and I try to spend about the same amount each week. When I've done this with some colleagues, informally, I've found that they waste about three times more time than they'd estimated for themselves. That's a lot of "lost" time, in which you could be doing other things to help achieve your success.

That perception is a big part of why I track my time, too. I don't want to run around thinking I'm wasting 30 minutes a day when in fact I'm burning three hours! Tracking my wasted time takes me out of the realm of *belief* and into the safer (for me) realm of *fact.* If I don't like the facts I find, I can make adjustments.

I also have a close-the-loop session toward the end of every day. If I scheduled an hour to work on a white paper, for example, then I just check myself at the end of the day. Did I get through it in an hour? Or did it take two hours? Was I interrupted in the middle and forced to re-set my mind, or did it just legitimately take two hours? The point of this isn't to punish myself, or even to try to make myself faster. Some things just take what they take. The point is to educate myself, to better understand how I work and how long things take. If I know that I can produce 2,000 written words in an hour, then I can start to make better estimates of how much work I can handle. If a new writing project comes in, I can see where on my schedule it will fit and have a more realistic estimate of when I can have that work done. This helps me set better expectations and do a better job of not promising something I can't deliver on. In the beginning, I kept a note on how long various common workloads would take me. For example, I know it takes me about six hours total to produce a slide deck for a one- to two-hour conference presentation. I know it takes about an hour to produce 2,000 written words, although I can only do that for about four hours before I need a solid break. These days, I've gotten so used to some of these that I don't need to refer to that note anymore, but it's still sitting on my computer someplace.

> I am amazed when people don't know how long it takes them to do something that is core to their existence. How could you not?

Time sometimes doesn't always go the way you want. For example, I've gotten out of bed some mornings planning to write 10,000 words or so during the day, and found myself utterly not in the mood. There's no point forcing it; I'd just write crap and have to start over later anyway. So I rearrange my schedule. I move some stuff into the current day that I'm more in the mood for, and find a place for that writing to happen. But the point is that I actually *rearrange* things. I don't just blow off the writing and hope I can squeeze it in someplace. I *manage* the problem, rather than ignoring it.

For me *managing time* isn't the same as *micro-managing time.* I'm not trying to tell myself what to do or force myself to be faster. I'm mainly *observing* the facts on the ground, and then building my planning process around that. It's kind of like gravity. I need to know how it works, so I don't hurt myself at the gym. Observing it and recording it doesn't mean I'm trying to change it; I'm just trying to get a handle around what I'm dealing with.

Communicate Well, Always

The ability to communicate, along with opposable thumbs, is one of the things that's set humans apart from other forms of life on Earth. Our ability to comprehend complex and abstract ideas and to then *communicate* those is what makes us special as a species. Look around you at *anyone* you consider successful, and you will see that they're usually an excellent communicator. If you're to be a Master, you will need to pass on information—and that means being able to communicate.

I'm going to share with you a transcript I made from a recent "communication" I had with a friend. We were at a bar, just talking. This isn't meant to pick on this one person; I meet *many* people who communicate in this fashion. I asked, and received, permission to record and transcribe this, and I've done so verbatim, changing only people's names.

Yeah, so, we're going out the other night. I was with Marty and Sharon. We went over to the Barley place down at Caesars. No, wait, it was at—what's the name of that place with the walkway? Is it the Flamingo? No, the Linq, that's it. Yeah, so we go over to the Barley place, and we're sitting down having wine— well, Sharon and I were, Marty doesn't like it so he just had beer. So Sharon is talking about what a crazy time she's having at work, and it turns out her boss used to work with Marty when he was over at B Gaming. No, he was at Caesars! Caesars, because Sharon's boss was there but when they shut down that PR department he had to move and that's how he got this job.

So, I'm guessing the takeaway here is, "Sharon works for someone who used to be Marty's boss." But there's a lot going wrong with this conversational style—and I'm not just picking on the "yeahs" and "sos;" I get that this was a casual conversation at a bar.

First, the storyteller here spends a significant amount of time trying to make sure he nails several details *that absolutely do not matter.* Details are important; I've written about that already. But when a detail *doesn't contribute anything meaningful to the story,* then you not only shouldn't worry about getting it right, *you should leave it out entirely.* Human brains, as I've written before, try to filter irrelevant information from your main stream of consciousness; when someone, in conversation, struggles with some detail and has to clarify it, then *your* brain assumes *it must be important.* From there, your brain kind of "holds" that information, looking for things to connect it to, to create an effective memory. In this case, the brain's been sent on a wild goose chase because none of these details *matter* and none of them will ever add up to something useful or noteworthy. **First lesson:** Omit details that aren't important to the story. *Think* about your story before you tell it so that you're not just reciting something but are actually *presenting* something.

Second, this story goes on far too long for what it is trying to convey. People are mortal creatures. We're all going to die, and we have a limited amount of time before that happens. Don't waste it. While extra detail can be useful in providing context and color, you don't want to go so overboard that you lose the attention of the people you're talking to. I see this happen *all the frakking time* in business situations! I know it seems like we're always trying to communicate *less,* with "elevator pitches" and "sound bites," and I don't want to advocate going overboard with that, either. But *think* about your story and make it *as short as it can be while conveying what it needs to.* **Second lesson:** Time is precious; don't waste it. Don't leave out *important* things, but really think about what adds value to your story before you start telling it.

Third, frankly, I don't give a crap about who Sharon does or does not work for. It has no impact on my life. It is information I will never use, much like whatever that class was I had to take every morning before Basic Computer Programming my senior year of high school. Literally, it might as well have been study hall because I can't remember a thing about it. **Third lesson:** Know your audience. Just as Stephen King's *It* is not suitable for 4 year-olds (OMG, clowns), not every story is suitable for every audience. Don't tell people things they can't use, act upon, or usefully pass on. This doesn't mean you should withhold information; just know what you expect your listeners to *do* with what you're telling them, and if you don't know what they're going to do with it, think hard about whether you want to inflict it upon them.

Finally, I *will* pick on the "yeahs" and "sos." Edit yourself. Most of the time, "um" and "er" words are a verbal tic that we use to fill an audible gap when our brain needs to catch up. Stop saying them. It's actually far more effective to *just remain silent* because that's an instinctive cue your listeners' brains will use to catch up themselves. You don't need to fill every moment with sound; Like the white space in a book or graphic, your pauses can help frame important points and provide a natural pacing to conversation. **Fourth lesson:** Ask friends, family, and colleagues to give you some signal—a raised finger, a hard eye blink, or something—whenever they catch you "um-ing." Listen to yourself do it. Don't apologize, because that creates a second unnecessary interruption in your story! Let people know that you won't acknowledge their signal, but *do* pay attention to it. Catch yourself, and just *pause* instead.

Concise. Only the details the matter. Stories told for the audience that's hearing them. No verbal "fillers." Communication is what sets us apart from the lesser beasts—be a great communicator.

Respect the Yellow Line

I know, I use a lot of Disney analogies in this book. In this case, what I love is that Disney recognizes that *familiarity breeds contempt*.

What Disney sells, in its theme parks, is *escape* and *entertainment*. It's not just about rides; it's also about an environment. In their lingo, it's a *show*, and shows, like all forms of fiction, require the willing suspension of disbelief. You *know* that princess is really just some college kid, but you *choose* to participate in the show and treat her like Cinderella or whatever. A maxim of fiction is that, in order for the audience to maintain their willing suspension of disbelief, you have to avoid chucking anything out-of-story at them, like a pissed-off janitor who just got dumped by her boyfriend the night before and who doesn't really want to be at work scraping gum off the asphalt this afternoon.

All of us have worked in an environment where one or more people just got too comfortable. Lord knows the Nevada Department of Motor Vehicles is well-equipped with people who forget why they're there. But you know what I mean here: that person who just brings all their baggage to work. They march in, plunk down, and make it clear that they're not happy to be there.

Every single day you set foot out of your home, you're engaging in a public performance. Everything you do affects everyone around you. That always-grumpy person isn't going to be first in line for a promotion because, honestly, everyone wishes they'd just quit and go do something else. A surly middle school teacher isn't going to be as effective as one that's in a better mood and who remembers why they're in that classroom in the first place. *Every day* is a performance where you're presenting your best self, even if that's not how you really feel right then. Every time you drop the performance and let people see through the facade, you're breaking the story. You're hurting everyone else's ability to continue suspending disbelief. You're damaging *your product.*

That's why, at Disney theme parks, there are yellow lines. At any possible place where an employee can come from "backstage" and into the sight of paying customers, there's a line on the ground in yellow traffic paint. It's a hard, visual reminder to *leave your shit here.* It's fine if you had a bad night last night. It's fine if you got dumped. It's fine if your cat died. It's fine if you can't pay your rent. Leave it all at the line, and it'll be there waiting for you when your shift is done. Because once you cross the line, the performance *is on.* You smile, you briefly remember *what you are being paid to do,* you buck up, and you go do it. "Past this line," they're taught, "you put on the performance and you don't break character. When you come back to the line, you can go back to being whomever you really are."

"Character." What an important word. In public, at work, we are all a character. We are playing a role. What is it that role needs to deliver? It doesn't really need to be *us;* we can be ourselves at home with friends and family.

What most of us lack, in life, is that yellow line. After going to the same office, the same job, the same co-workers day after day after day after day, we get complacent. We lose our respect for what we're there for. We forget *who we are supposed to be* at work, and we break character and drop our performance. *That's* when you damage Brand You. That's when your paying customer—your employer—gets to see behind the curtain. That's the precise moment when you take whatever seeds of success you've managed to plant there, and you crush those tender little shoots under your foot. That's when your career declines into a mere job, and where you stop investing in your future. It's where you damage your chances of ever truly becoming a Master.

So paint, in your mind, a yellow line. Perhaps it's just inside the front door of your home. Perhaps it's just outside the front door of your office. Wherever you paint it, mark it well. I'm serious: physically stand *at that location* and visualize a line, painted in thick, yellow, reflective traffic paint. Notice the scuff marks on it, where others have walked over it time and time again. Notice the little nicks along one edge where the UPS guy wheels his hand truck across it every day. Make it so real, in your mind, that you can't *not* see it every time you walk past that spot. Ask yourself how much longer it'll last before you need to touch it up. Make it *real.* And then respect it.

Every time you approach that line, *think about what it means.* Think about why you're at this location, and what you hope to achieve from it. How is this job helping your career? How is this helping you achieve your own success, and your own Mastery? How is this job enabling you to help others, either now or someday in the future? *What is the point of it all?* You don't need to be happy to be there— but you need to remember *why* you are there. Examine every bit of baggage that you've got with you right then. Enumerate them: cat died. Got dumped. Kid needs braces. Car door got dinged. *See* the baggage, pause at the yellow line, and *set down the baggage.* Nobody will touch it. It'll all be waiting for you when you come back out, but it has no place on the other side of the line. Your performance is about to begin: review your lines. Put a smile on your face. Raise the curtain, step onto stage, and *deliver.*

Own Your Own Life

Only you and yours can make good things happen for you, collectively.

Let's consider the difference between *job* and *career* as an example. Your employer owns your job; they pay you to perform a service. Your employer doesn't *owe* you anything other than the compensation you've already mutually agreed to. They don't owe you job training, unless they're asking you to do something new in your job. I've met a *lot* of people making $120k, $150k a year who moan that their employer won't send them to classes or conferences, even when the topic they're after doesn't really apply to anything their company is doing right then. *You* own your *career*. Your career is the thing that will get you your *next* job. You are responsible for feeding your own career, which may mean buying your own class or conference from time to time. "Well, why would I learn something new if my employer doesn't want to pay for it?" is very possibly the most naive, self-destructive, stupid thing I've ever heard a professional say out loud. If you're feeding your career, and that's put you in a place where you're now more skilled than your current job requires, then you *get a new job*. One that will pay for the skills you now have. You need, in other words to *own your own life*, even though your current employer may be partially subsidizing your current *situation*.

This is *personal responsibility*. Everything good and bad that happens to you is *on you*. It doesn't mean something bad is your fault, and it doesn't mean something good didn't come from someone else; it means that it's *on you* to deal with it. Life is something that you participate in, to be sure, but sometimes it's also something that *happens to you*. You didn't choose to get hit by that car, but now you have been, and where you go from there is *on you*. You didn't wreck the company and get everyone laid off, but whether or not you can easily get a new job is *on you.*

I once had a bad year with the IRS. Well, a couple of bad years. I was independent, and one year decided to send in the *exact* amount of estimated taxes I owed each quarter. The problem is that the calculation is actually recursive, and isn't finalized *until after the tax year is over.* So while it was arguably not my *fault* that I wound up owing over $20,000 in back taxes and penalties, it was *on me* to deal with it. I seriously considered just falling into the trap most people fall into, which is blaming the IRS and simply trying to ignore the problem. I fortunately did not. My family and I fell back to our "Oh Shit" budget, wherein we cut out *every* expense that wouldn't result in sickness or death. No TV. No eating out *for over a year.* Cheaper groceries. No road trips. Cancelled vacations. It was a *bad period* in my life, and I'm tensing up just writing about it. But regardless of the Congress that passed the laws and the IRS that enforced them, it was *on me* to fix, and so my family and I knuckled down and paid for my mistakes. We took on extra work, we did whatever was necessary to solve the problem. We got onto a payment plan with the IRS, took out a loan to cover what we needed, and just dealt with it.

This kind of personal responsibility doesn't need to be a big dramatic fallout with the IRS, by the way. It comes in every small thing you do every day. That report you turned in a day late. That person you pissed off in traffic because you cut them off. That little old lady you helped across the street. Good or bad, everything *in* your life is *on you.* If you're going to truly *drive* your own life, instead of just being a passenger, you have to *own* all of these things. Improve the ones you're not happy with, and exult in the ones you are, but *own* them all.

It may be that nobody helps you get ahead in your life. That's fine; life doesn't come with an assistance guarantee. Be the type of person who doesn't expect anyone's help. Be the type of person who vocally appreciates people who *do* help. Be the type of person who helps others, even if they don't say "thank you."

Bonus: On Being a Better Teacher

Nobody is born knowing how to teach; we have to be taught. Often times, we can learn through good examples but even then the actual "art of teaching" can be hard to observe. Let's break it down, and get you on the road to better teaching.

If you'd like further reading on the topic, check out *How We Learn: The Surprising Truth About When, Where, and Why It Happens* by Benedict Carey.

How Humans Learn

Learning is largely a function of memory. That is, when we experience something, and perhaps make a mistake, we form memories about that event and what we did. The human brain is wired to dislike failure, and so when we solve a problem, we tend to attach the memory of the solution to the memory of the problem. Therefore, when we encounter the problem again in the future, the solution is right there with it in our minds.

Our brains are constructed from specialized cells called *neurons*. These neurons are distributed across different sections of the brain, with each section managing something specific. There's the visual cortex, for example, which does most of the processing needed to let us see.

Neurons connect to each other through *synapses* to form *synaptic networks*. Those form the basis for our memories. When we experience something, the relevant neurons "light up," representing the visual, auditory, tactile, olfactory, and taste aspects of the experience. Non-sense knowledge also lights up neurons in the appropriate regions of the brain. The total collection of the synaptic network is, in essence, a *memory*. Memories can be weaker or stronger: a multi-sense experience that made a big emotional impact will often be stronger, whereas a single-sense experience that didn't make a big emotional impact will be weaker. Contrast a memory from a special time in your life with the memory of the person you just walked past on the street, and you'll understand the difference!

Recalling a memory also makes in stronger: "this is apparently useful," your brain thinks, "and so I'll keep it handy." A song you sing or hear a lot will be more "memorable" than one you've only heard once.

All of these built-in brain features started as survival mechanisms.

Memories have a kind of "survival of the fittest" action: the memories you use the most, which result in your continued survival, are the memories that pop up the most readily when you need them.

The Value of Repetition

Experiences aren't the only way we can learn, as any child who learned their "times tables" in school can remind you. If you just repeat something often enough, our brains' survival mechanism will kick in and make that memory accessible. Even today, I know that 9 times 4 is 54 mainly because my brain's survival mechanism was tricked, through endless repetition, into believing that memory was important.

But repetition can be used to strengthen *experiential* memories as well. Musicians rely on what they call "muscle memory" to play instruments. Their muscles don't actually have memories, of course; it's just the constant repetition during practice that makes those memories come up instantly. Their brains learn that "when I see this symbol on the page, I do *this* with the fingers."

Pounding facts into someone's head via repetition, especially for adults, is a horrible way to learn, mainly because most people hate repetition. It's why I personally can't do more than plunk out a basic tune on a piano: I don't have the patience to sit through the endless repetition that playing a piano would require. But that doesn't mean repetition doesn't have its place. If you're teaching someone something, eventually they'll come to the point where you want them to try doing it on their own. Some time later, make them do it again. And some time later, again. It doesn't need to be an every-single-day event, but forcing the brain to recall, filling in the bits it may have missed, and doing that every so often, will reinforce the memory and keep it sharp. After a time, there'll be no way to make the memory fade anymore... as anyone who's heard "it's a small world" can attest!

Getting in and Doing it

Because our memories can encompass abstract knowledge and facts along with sensory impressions, the memories with the most "factors" tend to be automatically stronger. Hearing someone tell you how to change the oil in a car is one thing. Watching a video of the process would be even better, because the visual cortex of the brain can get engaged, and because there'd likely be an audio element. But actually *doing it* on a real car involves touch, sight, sound, facts, smells, and if you're unlucky, taste. That's a combination that the brain won't soon forget.

That's one of the reasons apprenticeships have always been, in my mind, a more powerful way of learning than the "book smarts" most higher education programs focus on. In an apprenticeship, the apprentice *is right there in the thick of it* with their Master, and likely with skilled journeymen. They're creating powerful memories using not only abstract facts, but all five of their senses. *Reading* about being a blacksmith is a very different experience than actually pounding a piece of white-hot metal with a hammer.

When I was an aircraft mechanic apprentice, we *did* have classroom time. About once a quarter, we'd spend a week, or two at the most, learning the theory of the aircraft's design and operation. But then we went back to the shop floor and worked on those very same things. Nearly thirty years later, I can still cite some of the abstract, theory-of-operation facts I learned, because they're inextricably connected to some very vivid, sensory-based, hands-on memories. You only have to tear down an F-14 hydraulic mixer valve once before you have some *very* vivid memories, I assure you.

So get your apprentices *involved* as early, and as often, as possible. It's better to briefly explain what they're about to do, and then set them on it (supervising as necessary), than to try and explain *all* the background theory, *all* the tasks, and everything else up-front. Just get *in* it.

Why Analogies Work...
and How They Can Fail

Analogies are some of the most powerful ways we have to teach. The idea of an analogy is to take something the learner is already familiar with, and use it to explain something they're not.

For example, you're probably familiar with cars. In the world of computer programming, there's something called *object-oriented programming*, or OOP. Basically, OOP treats everything in the computer as an object, and an object is a lot like a car. Cars have properties, right? The make, model, color, engine size, and so on, are all *properties* of the car. Software objects have properties too, like the version number, the manufacturer name, and so on. As a programmer, you can examine those properties to learn about the object, and even change some of those properties to modify what the object does. Imagine being able to change the color of your car by just changing the "color" property—that's what you can do in software!

I've used a common analogy, there, to briefly explain part of a computer-y thing. One of the biggest values that you, as an individual person, can bring to your apprentices is a set of analogies that work for them. Everyone in the world has a different background, might be from a different culture, and has different past experiences; creating analogies that "speak" to a particular apprentice usually require someone who shares some of that same background, culture, and set of experiences. It's why *I* can't be a great teacher to *everyone;* I lack the diversity needed to construct analogies for everyone. What if you came from a culture were cars weren't common? Most of my analogies would fail. Teaching, in many respects, is nothing more than taking knowledge that someone else has created, which you have subsequently learned, and then "repackaging" that information into analogies that your particular audience will understand.

Be aware that all analogies, even (and perhaps most especially) the best ones, eventually fall apart. My software-objects-are-like-cars analogy will get you to a point in your understanding, but at some point the analogy quits working. Analogies often require us to oversimplify some aspects of what we're teaching, or require us to temporarily ignore certain details. That's *fine*. People can't learn All The Things all at once. So we can use analogies to get them past a certain point, and then either switch analogies to continue, or drop the analogies completely to continue. We can go back and revisit things: properties of software objects aren't *exactly* like the properties of a car. In software, you can have some properties that are *collections*, which means they can contain *other* objects. It's a bit like if your car had a "tires" property, which contained a collection of Tire objects that each represented a tire on the car. That's a fine approach, and it's important to keep in mind that analogies are meant to serve a purpose, and then be set aside.

The Importance of Sequencing

As you teach, it's really important to *sequence* what you teach.

 Okay, we're going to cook a meal. This is going to be a basic steak-and-potatoes meal, so we'll only have three or four main ingredients. You do need to be careful, because once we start, the stove is going to be hot, as will the pans we use. And at the end, you need to make sure you give the steak a few minutes to rest before you serve it, because it will actually still be cooking a bit when we take it off the heat. But first, we need to assemble our ingredients, and that's going to require you to learn to julienne a vegetable! But let me start by explaining the history of cattle husbandry in the United States.

That is so mis-sequenced that anyone listening to it would be completely justified in throwing up their hands and going to a restaurant to eat.

- Don't cover abstract concepts unless they directly relate to something *practical* that you are *just about to teach*. The history of cattle in the United States is not relevant to cooking a steak, so don't get into it now.
- Cover material *in the order a student would encounter it*. Start by setting up the ingredients. Teach them how to julienne as part of the prep process. Continue from there.
- Do not bring up cautions or warnings until *just before* they're relevant, like when you first turn on the stove or oven or

whatever. Otherwise, you're asking someone to remember an abstract fact, disconnected from any practical use, until later, when it suddenly becomes mission-critical. Human brains aren't good at that.

Also, don't forget that *you cannot prevent failure.* Not ever. You can't take this approach of, "I'm going to start by telling you all the things I wish I'd know before I made my first steak," because you're just stacking abstract facts rather than *getting into the task.*

 Hey, see there where your pan is smoking a lot? That's because you used the wrong kind of oil. Each oil has a different smoke point and flash point, and you need to use one that's suitable for the heat you're cooking with. Let's set that pan aside to cool, and start over.

That's a *perfect* example of controlled failure. Rather than make a big deal out of oil flash points and whatnot up front, you just let nature *safely* take its course. Once the *problem* occurs, you offer a solution. Human brains love problem-solution; they do not love solution-no-problem as much. We learn from mistakes, and so you need to sequence in the right mistakes so that the learner has an easier time ingesting all the info.

Why Rest Time is Crucial

Finally, remember that the human brain can physically only digest so much new information in a given period of time. If we're *doing* something with the information, as in getting hands-on with it right away, we can learn better, and learn more, in the course of a day. With abstract facts not connected to an activity or sensory experience, not so much—we're really limited. So rest time is crucial.

When we sleep, our brains reorganize our memories. Our brains decide which synapses get stronger, and which ones get marginalized, based on how we've been using those memories. New memories get connected to relevant older memories. We *need* time for this to occur.

That's yet another reason why I prefer apprentice-style learning to a week of all-day in-classroom learning. Apprentice-style learning builds better memories, and it spreads the learning out over a longer period of time, giving my brain more time to cope with the input. Classrooms can be a firehose of information with little connection to my real world, meaning I tend to forget a lot of what I learn.

Bonus 2: On Being a Master at Work

Mastery at work can be especially difficult to pull off, or at least non-obvious. But because that's where so many of us spend so much of our time, it's an attractive place to find an apprentice audience and help make changes in people's lives. With that in mind, I'll offer some observations and suggestions on the topic.

Initial Thoughts

For many of us, our most easily accessible and obvious audience of apprentices is at work, often in the form of junior colleagues. This part of the book is intended to help you address that audience and overcome the many challenges that often present themselves when you try to bring Mastery into the workplace.

I want to stress that *work isn't your only possible audience.* If you're really thinking *broadly* about the things you can teach, then it's always worth looking outside the workplace, too. Just because work is the easily accessible audience doesn't mean it's the best audience nor does it mean it's the place where you can have the most impact. Yes, teaching outside the workplace will mean extra time because you aren't teaching as part of your job, but sometimes that extra sacrifice is well worth it in the long run.

So even if work is the right place for you to start serving as Master, don't let it be the *last* place you serve.

The Pitch for Mastery at Work

There are a lot of good, and extremely valid, business reasons for reviving the old apprentice/Master relationship in the workplace.

First, all organizations suffer from a problem called *institutional memory*. This is the day-to-day "how we do stuff" that gets handed down from employee to employee but never gets documented. In reality, few organizations could afford to spend the time actually documenting every little detail of their business. For example, my first career was as an aircraft mechanic for the Navy. The Navy documents *everything*. I mean, Every. Thing. All the things. For one kind of airplane, we had an entire 2,000 square-foot room full of documentation. Even so, that documentation was rarely enough to actually put one of the damn things together. You had to know, for example, that the F-14's engine intake ramps couldn't be installed unless you greased the side seals with petrolatum and that you needed to use the white plastic side of the rubber mallet to beat them into place so that you could attach the actuators. Nobody documented those tidbits, but you literally couldn't do the job without them. That's why I was an *apprentice*, shepherded by several journeymen and Master mechanics who passed on those bits of lore. It was far cheaper, and more effective, to pass those bits of craft down through oral history than it was to expand the documentation by 20% to include all those little tips.

Second, although formal training in your craft has its place, it's not the best way to teach all things. Most carpenters' unions in the US, for example, have regional education facilities and teach continuing eduction classes for their members. These classes often focus on new materials, new code requirements, and so on. Those topics are often *best* taught in a formal setting like a class. But that doesn't stop the carpenters from maintaining their apprenticeships because the fine techniques of the craft are still best passed down on-the-job with an experienced journeyman or Master overseeing an apprentice. The same applies to any company.

Third, and this is a big one that a lot of organizations overlook, is *sustainability.* You know what one of the highest paying jobs in the information technology industry is? Mainframe programmer. It's not sexy, dealing with code originally written in the 1970s and 1980s, but it pays a lot because most of the people doing it are in their 60s, and companies are terrified that the only mainframe programmers on the planet are going to die any minute now. And it's a valid fear because *you basically can't get formal education* in mainframe programming anymore. Nobody runs classes. You can't even find teachers on the topic, in most places. Had these terrified companies engaged in apprenticeships a decade ago, though, they'd be fine. You see, your most senior people represent an immense investment and brain trust, but it's all locked up in their brains. If you don't let them - nay, *demand* that they - pass it on, then at some point, you're going to lose all that and have to start over.

> As an aside, let me stress that I'm blaming *companies* for their mainframe programming woes because they didn't *insist* on their programmers bringing in new blood. That also includes those companies ensuring their Masters weren't being made to feel like training up new blood would put themselves out of a job just a couple of years before retirement.

I spent some time working for Electronics Boutique, which was later known as EB Games, which was purchased by a company called Game Stop (I point this out only in case you've heard of one of them). When I started at EB, as we called it, I was a lowly sales associate. But my store manager had a very "apprenticeship" mindset. She didn't have the "key holder" concept that a lot of small retail stores do, wherein only a few trusted individuals are allowed to open or close the store. *Everyone* in our store, even most of our seasonal part-timers, knew how to do *everything* in the store. Stocking. Cleaning. Opening paperwork. Returns. Closing paperwork. Everything. Much of it was documented in writing, but plenty of it was handed down from other employees. As a result, *we were all easily promotable* elsewhere in the company, and our store was in fact known as a place that new assistant managers came from. When someone left, the manager didn't have to rush to replace them because we all knew how to do every job. The company benefitted massively in both the small scale and large because of her attitude.

What amazes me is that more organizations don't *insist* on having Mastery be a part of the workplace.

Hurdles to Mastery at Work

Companies don't always understand the benefits of making Mastery and apprenticeships part of the workplace. In writing this book, I reached out to friends and colleagues and asked what hurdles they'd run into. I'll use their (unattributed and somewhat edited) quotes to drive some of this conversation.

Fear

This is a common personal objection, and it's one I've seen those aforementioned mainframe programmers deploy:

> I'm one of very few people who does what I do in my company, and if I train up new people, I'm just begging for them to replace me when I'm no longer needed.

First, let's acknowledge that your company needs to provide you with some assurances that you're not going to be let go once you've trained up some apprentices. That's a very valid thing to just ask them for, straight-out. Mastery shouldn't end in you losing your livelihood before you're ready. One way some companies address that is to create a dedicated "trainer" position for a senior person who continues to work but focuses heavily on bringing in a new generation.

Second, let's acknowledge the toxic situation *you create for yourself* when your sole claim to job security is that you've got some unique information locked up in your head that you're reluctant to share. *You* should be doing more to ensure your *career security* for yourself. If you're close to retirement and just trying to eke out a few more years without having to learn something new, *then your company is probably right to want to replace you.* You can, and should, do more to ensure your own continued viability in your field. I apologize if this comes across as insensitive; I don't mean it to, and sometimes it's difficult to convey subtle emotions in writing. But I do think there's more than one perspective to consider with this kind of objection. If your main value-add at work is that *you're the only one* (or one of a few) *who knows something*, then I feel you've made poor career choices and you should rectify that. Hoarding job skills is essentially holding your employer at ransom, and that's never a healthy relationship.

Think about a slightly different perspective: As your employer, I know you have these job skills and knowledge locked up in your head. I also know that you'll leave the company one day, for some reason. If you're not willing to help train up new talent now, then I've no reason to suspect you'll be willing in the future. That means my life, as an employer, is going to suck whenever you leave because we've both conspired to make you hard to replace. Ergo, I might as well rip the bandage off and let you go *now*, so I can get the suck out of the way and move on with the business. In other words, there's a very real argument that if you're not helping to move the craft along, then I might as well lose you sooner rather than later.

All of this presumes that your employer is pushing you to take on apprentices, and that isn't always the case. As I pointed out in the earlier example, I feel companies should *insist* on Mastery in the workplace, particularly when they have a small group of potential Masters who have a lot locked up in their brains that the company depends on.

Time

Here's one of the most common organizational objections:

> The objection I've run into is, "If we let people become mentors, they won't have time to do the job they were hired for."

I hear this a lot myself, and it's especially common in the US, with our nose-to-the-grindstone, profit-minding mindset. I approach it in few ways:

- Don't think of mentoring as a time-suck, think of it as a force multiplier. If the person doing the mentoring is being paid more than the people they're mentoring, then it's a way to get those lesser-paid people *doing more*. Suddenly, that one mentor can do the work of many people because they've created apprentices and journeymen to help out. Perhaps those apprentices and journeymen will demand more pay at some point, but the business can decide at that time if they've room for more productive, more effective employees. The right mentor can reduce or eliminate the need to hire.
- If the counter-argument becomes, "We don't want to teach people more because then they'll want more money and we don't want to pay them," then you need to seriously consider the life choices that led you to work for a company *that actively wants to hold back people from personal and professional growth.* This is not an organization that will "have your back," and you might point out how that's going to look to people.
- Mentoring is the best way to get employees to work, and behave, the way the organization most wants them to. It's a way of preserving the "institutional memory" that all organizations have - the stuff they never write down but can't run

without. You can't hire people who know exactly how you want things done, but you *can* raise them that way. Mentors can also pass down better work ethics, and companies that engage in mentoring tend to have lower turnover and higher overall productivity.

- If mentoring is something that *you*, in your career, are ready for, and if it's part of how you define yourself and define your success, share that with your organization. Let them know that although you value your position, *you* need to have mentoring become a part of it. You don't need to make this a threat of quitting, but make it clear that *you* need things from your job, and you're willing to incorporate those things with their permission.
- Address the time-suck problem head-on. Ask for two hours a week, or some other reasonable, nominal amount of time. *Track* that time, and make the most of it. Track your results, too: Are you able to point to improved performance, broader job responsibilities, or other growth in the people you're mentoring? That can help show that the investment—those few hours a week—is generating a return, and open the door to further investment.

More broadly, start to ask, *"Why aren't we hiring people who can be mentors to our teams?"* It seems like one of the most obvious things to *want* to have on staff, so why isn't it built right into the job description of more senior-level employees? How much more self-sustaining and stable would the company be if it embraced a culture of education and helping without having to constantly spend money having *outsiders* do that training? Especially when outsiders *don't know the company* as well as its own employees do?

If the real fear is, "We're afraid that you'll *only* be teaching and won't do *any* of your original job," then *manage* that. Schedule and assign teaching time like any other task. Track it, track the results, and start building a culture of mentorship.

The Optics

This particular quote is most obviously applicable to consulting companies, but it has meaning to other kinds of organizations, too:

> We really embrace mentoring. The problem is that while on a customer site, it's hard to be seen mentoring your own team when you're all on the customer's dime. So we now mentor customers' employees and our own team members, at the same time.

This is so brilliant I almost don't even know what else to say. But what's really happening here is someone learning to *expand their apprentice audience*. It's definitely tackling a problem head-on, too, which I'm a big fan of. "Hey, we want to mentor our people, but it's making us look kind of awkward." Well, okay, let's engage in some empathy: What exactly is the customers' problem? Where is the awkwardness coming from? The problem is that they feel they're being charged to train the consultants that they hired. So the ultimate problem is that the customer feels like they're paying for something they're not getting. Fine, let's give them something! We'll mentor their people, too, which is both objectively valuable *and* shows that we're okay with them becoming more self-sufficient and reducing their reliance on us as consultants. This is an incredibly professional and forward-thinking approach that probably wins the consulting company *more* business.

Mastery in the Workplace in Three Straightforward Steps

I'm all about being as prescriptive and actionable as possible, so let's see if we can't create a straightforward path toward bringing Mastery into the workplace.

Step 1: Start Small

If you organization doesn't already have an apprentice/Master or mentoring culture, then you're going to want for it to be seen, at least initially, as an experiment. Experiments almost always start out small. They're tightly scoped so that you can reduce the number of variables you have to deal with and focus the experiment on just the one thing you're trying out. They're also small because that helps reduce the area of effect if the experiment fails.

So think of formally mentoring *one person*, or maybe a very small team of people, at the most. And figure out some specific thing that you're going to help teach them; don't make mentoring some kind of open-ended, vague project. Specificity lends itself to measurability, and measuring an experiment is how you determine whether it was a success. As you're figuring out what you'll be teaching your new apprentice(s), keep in mind that you want the timeframe for the experiment to be relatively small, too, perhaps a month or two. Three months at the outside, and even that only because so many businesses are accustomed to dealing with organizational objectives and goals on a quarterly basis.

Make sure your plan accommodates your company's culture and structure. For example, imagine you work for an airline, and you work in the customer service group that mans the phone lines customers call in on. You've noticed that certain types of calls, often dealing with requests for ticket refunds, always have to involve a supervisor. The supervisors have a fairly complex rule set that determines when they're allowed to issue a refund, and you're thinking that you could teach that rule set to the front-line phone-answerers. It'd help those folks understand the business better, it'd smooth out customers calls, and it'd help reduce the workload on the supervisors. Sounds great!

Except that the airline likely has other reasons for the supervisors being involved. It might be to make the refund process *seem* harder on purpose so that customers are less likely to engage that process frivolously. It might be that there are internal financial and loss-prevention rules that mandate a supervisor's involvement. What you don't want to do is try to solve a problem by moving *authority* to someone else in the organization because that creates another even more difficult set of problems and will likely result in your Mastery experiment failing altogether.

Step 2: Make a Plan

When I think "uncontrolled experiment," I imagine exploding vats of acid. *Uncontrolled* is often seen as a bad word within organizations, so you certainly don't want your Mastery experiment seen as uncontrolled. That means you need a plan.

Your plan needs to include a few basic pieces of information:

- What's the goal of the experiment, in as much specificity as possible? To whom are you proposing to teach what?
- What's the timeframe for the experiment?

- At the end of the experiment, what objective criteria will determine whether it was a failure, a success, or inconclusive? *Objective criteria* are things anyone could look at and agree upon, like an apprentice's newfound ability to perform tasks they weren't able to do previously.

Your plan also needs to include a business justification, meaning you need to detail why *the business itself* should want the experiment to succeed. This justification will nearly always be money-based, because money is one of the few objective measurements a business can make about itself.

For example, let's run the math equation I mapped out earlier in the book. Look at your proposed apprentice audience, and estimate how much they make per year. Oftentimes, your company's Human Resources (or equivalent) department can give you a predefined salary range for a job role without compromising anyone's privacy. Take that salary and multiply it by 1.4 for a rough[2] *fully loaded salary* estimate. Divide that by 2,000 for a rough hourly wage.

Now look at whatever it is you're proposing to teach to your apprentice(s). Are you proposing something that will eventually save them time or make them more efficient? Then measure *their current time or efficiency* in hours spent per year, and multiply that value by the rough hourly wage you calculated earlier. So, if your apprentices spend about 100 hours a year doing something, and they make $25 an hour fully loaded, then your current spend is about $2500 per person per year.

How much time are you proposing to save by teaching them something? Run the math on the new anticipated spend. Perhaps you're proposing to make them doubly efficient in this task, taking the spend down to $1300 per person per year, for a $1200 annual savings. That might not seem like much, but bear in mind that your Mastery experiment is deliberately small, so you would expect it

---

[2]This is a fairly conservative number in the US. Some companies use multipliers from 1.8 to 2.2, so you might ask your HR department what they use to estimate a fully loaded salary.

to have small returns on investment. The other side of that is that the experiment's *downside*, should it fail, will be equally small. Meaning you, as the proposed Master in the experiment, won't be investing a huge amount of your own time to try to realize that $1200 return, and so if the return is never realized, then the money invested won't have been large, either.

Your plan also needs to include the amount of time *you* plan to invest, expressed as money from your own fully loaded salary calculation.

If you're having trouble coming up with those monetary numbers, then your plan is probably not specific enough and not outcome-based enough. For example, I work in the technology industry, mostly with a product called Windows PowerShell. It's basically a programming language, and it tends to be used by more-senior people who design and operate computer networks and server infrastructure. I have plenty of colleagues who would love to do internal classes in their company and teach Windows PowerShell to their less-experienced colleagues. That's great, but it makes a horrible Mastery experiment. Windows PowerShell itself is a *tool* not a business outcome. It's like saying you'd like to teach hammers to a group of your colleagues. Hammers are great, but they are not, in and of themselves, a business outcome. So it's hard to think of how much hammers might save the company in monetary terms.

The trick is to get *task-based*. "My team needs to build walls out of 2x4 lumber, and they currently use rocks, which takes forever and causes a lot of busted thumbs. It currently takes one person almost 4 hours per wall, with an average of one injury per wall. Those injuries, and that time, cost us money. I propose to teach a new way of building walls that uses hammers. It'll be three times as efficient, and should reduce injuries by 90%." That's a business outcome. Yes, you're still teaching hammers, but you're doing so in a very specific, outcome-based context that has business value attached to it. "I'm going to invest eight hours of my own time, split across four two-hour sessions, which will each take place on

Tuesdays for a month." This is a tightly scoped plan, and you can see where it's easy to attach financial numbers. It's also easy to measure the outcome, once your experiment is complete, by using a stopwatch and by measuring injuries over the following month.

Step 3: Sell and Execute

The last step, of course, is to get permission. The more tightly scoped and objectively measurable your plan is, the easier it'll be to get it approved. And then you simply have to *execute* the plan. If you were extremely specific with the plan itself, then the execution should seem clear and straightforward.

When the experiment concludes, be sure to follow up. Write up a report that restates the problem you were trying to solve, explain what was invested in the experiment, and report on the measured outcomes. Conclude your report with a suggested plan of action, which might be a second, larger-scale experiment or a longer-running mentoring project. Have that next step lined up and ready to go. Even if your first experiment failed, analyze why, and propose a follow-on, small-scale experiment that attempts to correct whatever problems you ran into previously.

And, in Closing

Well. I certainly hope all that has helped a little, or if nothing else, maybe given you a new perspective to consider. I'd like to leave you with just one thought.

A Closing Thought

I've tried to make a big deal out of a *Master* being someone who teaches, someone who passes on what they know, and someone who helps bring along another generation into their craft. A Master doesn't necessarily know it all, and a Master is constantly learning (or should be). You *already* hold within you enough expertise to be a Master to someone, in some topic; you just need to find your apprentices. That may require you to first find some personal success and to build your personal confidence—that's well and good. Just know that you're already "worthy." A Master isn't an expert; a Master is someone with an apprentice.

But perhaps I started this book with an assumption that you'd *want* to be this kind of person without giving you a good reason *why*. After all, for most of us, passing on what we know doesn't generate any direct personal reward. Sure, maybe it gets some people to admire us, which feels nice, but at the end of the day, what's the upside?

This is where I have to appeal to some of the selflessness that you doubtless hold inside of you. Imagine working in a field, or indeed living in a world, where we not only helped our peers and colleagues from day to day but also *actively* "looked back" and helped the people who were a bit "behind" us in our field. Imagine what a culture we could create, bringing folks into and further into our field. A newcomer to your "craft" wouldn't know any other way, and they'd be encouraged to eventually do the same. We'd all just be people, helping each other in small ways to earn success. Maybe none of us would become famous for it, but how wonderful a life would that help create?

What if, in time, we could recreate the apprenticeships and guilds of old? We wouldn't need to rely on the whims and needs of our individual organizations to further our trades or to ensure new people were ready to take their places in them. Businesses needing skilled workers at all levels could simply turn to the appropriate guild to find entry-level workers, journeymen, and Masters. We, as tradespeople, would take care of each other, share our knowledge and experiences, and vouch for each others' expertise. Our success is *all of our* successes.

Hey, a guy can dream.

Thanks for reading.

Afterword

As with many books, this one has been a labor of love. And not just my love for writing, although that's a big part of it. It's also a love born from the deep respect I have for the communities I've been part of. You know, it's funny, but if you watch basically any news channel at all, you can easily come away with the idea that we live in a hostile world full of hostile people. But that's not really the case. Every single day I meet, speak to, and work with incredible, kind, genuine people. Many of them have done well for themselves but feel that they could be doing more for others. Some struggle just to get their own lives on the track they want. It's for all of them that this book was written, in a hope that, in some small, tiny way, it can give them a thought or two toward reaching their own goals.

Keep in Touch

I hope you'll let me know what you think of the book. I'm easy to reach through the "Hit Me Up" link on my blog at DonJones.com and on Twitter @concentrateddon. Even if you're just pointing out a typo, I appreciate hearing from you.

As a note, references to the book should include a heading and paragraph number when possible; the page numbers you see don't correspond at all to my source material, so they're not useful in tracking down whatever you've written to me about.

Know that I adore your feedback. I hang on every word, and it directly influences future editions of this book as well as all my other work. So long as you're giving me something actionable to consider, I'll do my best to understand it, let it change my own perspective, and let that come out in future works.

I also adore your honest reviews on Amazon and other bookseller websites. Those go a long way toward helping other people decide to make a purchasing decision, and taking that time to help someone else is a great gift. If you've written a critical review, I hope you've packed in as much detail as possible so that I can attempt to address your concerns in a future revision or Edition (and remember, Leanpub purchases get future revisions of this same Edition at no extra charge).

Finally, knowing full well that you'll find your own success and your own path to it, I hope that—as you do so—you'll share. Write your own version of this book or even just a blog about your journey. It'll help *someone* out there, I promise.

Acknowledgements

I want to thank everyone who's provided feedback, suggestions, and corrections. I also want to especially thank Laurie Wells, who painstakingly copyedited the previous edition, much of which has carried over to this one. Any remaining mistakes are definitely mine, though.

Suggested Reading

If you're going to teach, then it's worth spending some time understanding how people learn. For me, *How We Learn* by Benedict Carey is a perfect way to do that. More cognitive science than instructional design, Carey manages to avoid the utter condescension that most books on the topic have, while keeping it real-world and relatable, unlike most of the *rest* of books on the topic.

The Nine Principles of Immediately Effective Instruction is my own work and is more about how to create instructional materials. It's free on my website[3], so if it's not really applicable to your life, then at least it didn't cost much. I've also written *Instructional Design for Mortals* if you're interested in learning how to create better learning materials without getting a Doctorate in the subject. That can be found on Leanpub as well as on Amazon, and I've linked on the Books page at DonJones.com.

I tend to *hate* "how to succeed in business"-type books. I mean *Seven Habits* and other popular tomes notwithstanding, they just don't tend to speak to me. That said, I did enjoy *Superbosses: How Exceptional Leaders Master the Flow of Talent* by Sydney Finkelstein. It helped me observe productive and counterproductive behaviors of my own, and adjust accordingly.

Despite this book's obvious intent, I'm also not much on self-help books. I have, however, gotten some good bits from *Hacking Laziness: How to Outwit, Outsmart & Outmaneuver Procrastination* by Mike Buffington and *Habit Stacking: 127 Small Changes to Improve Your Health, Wealth, and Happiness* by S. J. Scott, both of which are conveniently on Kindle Unlimited, if you have that.

---

[3]https://donjones.com/2014/01/05/free-the-nine-principles-of-immediately-effective-instruction/

Kindle Unlimited is totally evil, by the way. Ask me about it in a bar sometime.

Finally, *Dragonflight* is just the best damn sci-fi book I've ever owned. And it *is* sci-fi, not fantasy. And, I just recently learned that it was just inches shy of becoming a television program, and its failure to do so is largely why we got the 2003 *Battlestar Galactica* reboot that we did. Pick up a copy of *So Say We All* for that story.

Made in the USA
Lexington, KY
12 December 2019